Parental Presence

Parental Presence

Reclaiming a Leadership Role in Bringing Up Our Children

◆

Haim Omer

ZEIG, TUCKER & CO., INC.
PHOENIX, ARIZONA

I dedicate this book to my five children:
Nati, Yonathan, Michael, Noam, and Yael

◆

**Note: The names and details of the cases presented have
been changed to protect the confidentiality of the clients.**

Library of Congress Cataloging-in-Publication Data

Omer, Haim.
    Parental presence : reclaiming a leadership role in bringing up
our children / Haim Omer.
        p. cm.
    Includes bibliographical references and index.
    ISBN 1-891944-39-8
    1. Discipline of children. 2. Discipline of children—Psycho-
logical aspects. I. Title.
HQ770.4.O45 1999
649'.64—dc21
                                                    99-034352

Published by
ZEIG, TUCKER & CO., INC.
3618 North 24 Street
Phoenix, Arizona 85016

Manufactured in the United States of America

Designed by Kathleen Lake, Neuwirth & Associates

10 9 8 7 6 5 4 3 2 1

Contents

Contents

Introduction

There are countless ways of bringing up children. The variety of extant family structures, values, and practices defies categorization. The present generation has witnessed the appearance and diffusion of family constellations that would have been considered unacceptable just a few decades ago. And yet children from highly unconventional family structures can grow up to be well-adjusted adults. Gone is the age where one could pontificate on *the* right way of parenting or argue *the* best family structure. However, even in our modern Tower of Babel of family forms, there is one firm agreement shared by all caring parents: they don't want their children to use drugs, resort to violence, engage in criminal acts, or become promiscuous. To put it positively, all parents want to be able to convey their standards and values and to have their children grow up to be human beings whom they will appreciate—people who will contribute to society. Parental authority is this ability to establish rules and values for the child and to prevent all actions that subvert them. In this sense, all parents, be they modern or old-fashioned, lay or religious, honest or dishonest, want to possess authority. They may prefer to back their authority by blind obedience or rational discussion, by prize or punishment, by positive example ("Do as I do!") or negative example ("Don't do as they do!"); however, without authority they cannot hope to have their standards prevail or to prevent their children from destroying themselves.

This book is about parents who have lost their authority in families where the flouting of parental rules is the norm—where the children or adolescents hold sway by means of threats, violence, blackmail, indifference, and withdrawal. The purpose of this book is to present principles and tools for the recovery of parental authority in such families.

This book takes the pluralism of modern society as a given. It is not a call to return to traditional values as a panacea for our problems. Neither does it presume to present a right or better way of rearing children. What is right and good for one family or child may be wrong for another. However, when the parents feel helpless in the face of a child's violence and self-destructiveness, change is a necessity. Then we are justified in working toward the recovery of parental authority. It is precisely in such dire situations that parents often ask for professional help. Unfortunately, we professionals have not always been helpful.

I believe that parents have often been treated unkindly by the helping professions. They have been made to take the blame for every problem posed or faced by their children. They have been accused of serving their own egotistic (*narcissistic*, in psychological jargon) ends rather than the needs of their children. They have been routinely described as lacking in empathy and sensitivity and as having only minimal understanding of their children. They have been told that children are so delicate and vulnerable that the slightest mistake in parenting will leave indelible scars. Professionals have often maintained that the healing of such scars is the exclusive province of the therapist, but almost simultaneously they imply that therapy can only be of help if parents change their attitude toward the child.

However, this required change is hazily defined. It is not a specific change in behavior, but an inner one: the mother, for instance, should become more "motherly." Actually, what is expected is that she become like the therapist: a good mother should be accepting, warm, empathic, sensitive, nonjudgmental, nondemanding, and nonpunishing. The mother then finds it difficult to compete with the therapist on these terms. The upshot of the professional encounter is that the parents are left feeling even more incompetent, weak, and guilty. Rather than strengthening parental authority, some professionals instead help to undermine it.

But am I missing the point? Might it be that the problem is not due to a lack of authority, but to a lack of acceptance and warmth? Might it be that by furthering authority measures, we end up aggravating the very situation we set out to remedy? That our very focus on authority reflects a failure to create the optimal permissive environment for the child's growth? Indeed, these ideas have been highly influential and at the time that they were popular they constituted the bible of child rearing. Today, we know that the dream of total permissiveness has proved hollow (Baumrind, 1971, 1991). Children reared in such families are no less liable to conduct disorders, violence, and delinquency. Actually, they are *more* liable. In addition, they suffer from very low self-esteem.

This robust research finding shakes the permissive ideology to its roots. Indeed, the gist of the permissive dream is a vision of children who develop their own resources and aptitudes without external warping. Children thus brought up should turn out to be self-assured, open-minded, creative, and resilient. Research has shown that it is not so: children reared without limits and demands often grow up with no sense of worth, little ability to withstand frustration, and a total lack of inner direction. The absence of limits and demands has thus proved no less warping than has the most rigid authoritarianism.

Are we then back to the old ways in which the parent knows best and the father who spares the rod hates his child? Not at all.

These same studies have shown extremely rigid and dogmatic parenting to be as bad for the child as total permissiveness. Needless to say, physical violence against children has disastrous results. However, we should keep in mind that the child's violence may have equally disastrous consequences. Indeed, it is the best predictor of adolescent violence, which, in turn, is the best predictor of adult violence and criminality (Chamberlain & Patterson, 1995; Patterson, Reid, & Dishion, 1992). Children will thus suffer from violence in the home, whether its victims or its perpetrators. Therefore, the major goal is a home atmosphere that is free of violence by children and parents alike. Paradoxically, parental violence against children is often the result of a failure in authority: it is the resourceless parent who may be most at the mercy of violent impulses when feeling harassed by a child he or she does not know how to manage. In helping the helpless parent to recover control, we will also be furthering parental *self*-control.

Important lessons learned from research on parenting are somewhat thwarting to parents and professionals alike: universal rules are not to be had, absolute ideologies of child rearing disappoint, what works with one child often fails with another, and there are no sure ways to prevent mistakes. Then how can we presume to be of help? Where can we find a starting point?

Most people agree that to bring up well-adjusted and well-behaved children, we need a proper blend of firmness and love. The problem is that this blend is pulled apart when children have serious behavioral problems. Parents tend to be either too loving or too firm or they alternately swing between the two extremes. And so do professionals: some are champions of warmth and acceptance, others of rules and boundaries. Again, many hold both to be necessary, but with no clear answer as to how to make them work together. Although the issue is not critical with less demanding children, it is crucial for the extremely unruly or violent: they require so much firmness that the parental expression of love is hardened and are often so needy of love that parental firmness is melted. The loving extreme of parental interaction then takes the form of compensation, which undermines the previous firmness; this is followed by the opposite extreme of firmness, which now takes the form of punitive rejection, thereby obliterating the experience of love. This book is an attempt to put forth the guiding concept of *parental presence*, so as to unify firmness and love, and create a legitimate kind of parental authority.

The book covers the many facets of parental presence. Chapter 1 ("Parental Presence Defined") introduces and illustrates the concept. Chapter 2 ("Parental Presence in the Light of Other Approaches") analyzes the concept of parental presence in light of behavioral, systemic, and humanistic approaches.* Chapter 3 ("Behavioral Presence") describes how parents may recover the capacity to act. Chapter 4 ("Systemic Presence") deals with the positive and negative impact of others (e.g., the spouse, the school, the extended family, and the child's peers) on parental presence.

Chapter 5 ("Personal Presence") describes the loss and retrieval of the parent's personal voice as an individual human being. Chapter 6 ("Flexible Authority") deals with impasse and its resolution. Chapter 7 ("Involving the Child in the Therapy") presents some positive ways of involving the child in the therapy without weakening the parents. The book ends with an evaluation of whether parental presence meets the practical, theoretical, and ethical criteria that would make the concept acceptable to parents and professionals alike.

Most important from our point of view is the inclusion, throughout the book, of cases that were not fully successfully resolved and of treatment complications that led to difficult impasses. One of the cases presented was a downright failure. We

---

*This chapter may be skipped by the nonprofessional reader.

think that professional honesty and credibility suffer from the fashionable presentation of magical, invariably successful, therapies. Such a bias leaves professionals and parents unprepared for impasse and failure.

Acknowledgments

This book would have been a much more difficult undertaking were it not for the help of Uri Weinblatt. He started the project with me (we began with an ad in the newspaper inviting "Parents Who Fear Their Children" to volunteer for a trial counseling program). Many of the cases in the book were treated by him. He also coauthored Chapter 2. When I write in the first person plural, this is no mere stylistic usage: the *we* refers to all the therapists who worked under my supervision and, especially, to Uri Weinblatt, who played a key role in developing the model. I thank him deeply.

I also want to thank the many parents who allowed me to share their sufferings and triumphs and all the therapists who worked under my supervision. I had initially thought about dedicating this book "to my five children, who taught me all I know about parental helplessness." But since they also taught me many other things, better and more pleasant, I simply dedicate it to them— period.

◆

Parental Presence Defined

We all know that one of the worst traumas for a child is to grow up without a caring person in his or her life. We also know that the loss of a parent, even in later childhood, may be devastating. Less recognized, however, is another form of deprivation: that experienced when a parent "collapses," becomes paralyzed, or loses his or her personal voice. Parents often give in when faced with the child's demands, complaints, threats, or aggression. However, when giving in becomes the norm, the child becomes deprived of *parental presence*. What is perhaps worse is that the child feels that he or she has abolished the parents' presence.

The parents' experience in the same circumstances may be the very opposite: they may feel that they exist only for the child. But that is precisely the problem: if the parent exists only for the child, the parent has no voice and no individuality. The parent then becomes the executor of the child's will, the child's servant, the child's shadow. To be present is to be somebody, with one's own thoughts, feelings, and wants. In order to grow up, the child needs such a somebody. Only with a figure who is personally present can the child feel secure and not alone. In contrast, the parent who becomes the echo of the child's wishes leaves the child in a vacuum.

The experience of parental presence may also become flawed in another respect: when the child is faced with a caretaker who is present as an individual, but not as the fulfiller of the parenting role. Some parents turn this into an ideal: "I want to be my son's friend" or "I want to be loved for what I am and not because I am her mother." Other parents neglect the parental role by simply asserting their own needs with no consideration for those of the child. In both cases, the child misses the presence of the parent *qua* parent.

Parental presence is thus a bipolar concept: the parent must be present both as an individual and as the incumbent in the parenting role. If either of the two is lacking, the child will suffer deprivation. The worst deprivation, however, is occasioned by a figure who has become effaced both as a person and as a parent.

The Practical, Conceptual, and Ethical Levels of Parental Presence

The concept of parental presence must meet a triple challenge: (1) on a practical level, it must provide one with simple guidelines that allow for quick decisions under emotional pressure; (2) on a conceptual level, it must serve as a bridge between workers with different views and approaches; and (3) on an ethical level, it must further an acceptable brand of authority, clearly distinct from one based on naked power.

The practical criterion derives from the urgency of the problems with which we are dealing. Violence, suicide threats, and running away call for immediate action. Thus our concept should be able to provide us with emergency responses, as well as with longer-term solutions. I hope to show that the model of parental presence allows for an intuitive grasp of burning issues, as well for the development of farsighted plans.

The conceptual criterion follows from the frequent need to involve different parties (parents, school staff, police officers, therapists, social workers) in the treatment of each case. Our concept should be acceptable to these many parties, helping them to understand each other, so as best to work out a common plan. I hope to show that parental presence may serve not only as a bridge between behavioral, systemic, and humanistic approaches, but also as a rallying cry to parents and educators.

The ethical criterion has to do with the legitimacy of the proposed measures. But, legitimacy according to whom? Various perspectives should be taken into account. Obviously, the measures should be legitimate in the eyes of the law. In some countries, for instance, even holding a child against his or her will is against the law. Professionals will then have to take into consideration whatever legal constraints are locally operant. The authority measures should also be legitimate in the parents' eyes. Therapists will then have to match their ideas to the parents' mores. It is legitimate, of course, to negotiate with the parents, trying to bring them over to one's point of view. In the end, however, only what the parents fully accept can be viewed as a valid step.

I also deem it vital that the measures be viewed as acceptable by the professionals involved with a case (therapists, social workers, teachers). I would venture that any approach that runs counter to the judgment of these professionals stands little chance of being consistently embraced by the parents. And what about the children? Must not the measures also be acceptable to them. No; not from the very start. Children of all ages will try to shake off any authority that limits the freedom to which they are accustomed. If, however, the children cannot grow to accept the steps, but persist in viewing them as totally illegitimate, something is wrong with the proposed measures and they will have to be modified.

Parental presence will be our touchstone for evaluating authority measures: Does the measure under consideration confer a sense of stable presence or does it work only as a form of crude and distant power? For instance, both the parent who spanks and chases the child and the parent who withdraws as a form of punishment are failing the presence test: spanking is the least possible contact, taking but a fraction of a second, and parental self-withdrawal is a form of absence. Also, the parent whose relationship with the child becomes reduced to a stereotyped power struggle, in which each move by the child leads to a totally predictable countermove by the parent and vice versa, will be failing the presence test: such a parent behaves, and appears to the child, as a one-dimensional caricature rather than as a real person.

But might not the child be suffering from an excess of parental presence—and increasing it will only stifle his or her burgeoning individuality? Indeed, as the child grows, parents must learn to step back, making their presence less and less prominent. Failing this, the child may remain dependent and immature. But what is the right pace for stepping back? For how long should the parents' involvement and supervisory activity be maintained? Most would agree that so long as the child lives under the parental roof, the parents should be able to reassert their presence whenever violence erupts or when the child's safety is at risk. In the families with which we are dealing, this parental ability is badly compromised: the parents are so paralyzed that they have lost the capacity to protect either themselves or the child.

The Foundations of Parental Presence

There are three aspects to parental presence.

1. The parents must become able to undertake effective action,
2. develop a sense of moral and personal confidence,
3. and feel that their efforts are supported rather than undermined by others.

In other words, the parents must be able to say: "I can act!" "This is right!" "I am not alone!" These are the three foundations of parental presence. The first brings the parents back to the family stage as agents; the second, as moral and individual beings; the third, as parts of a supportive context. The three are intimately related: the power to act stems from the parents' personal and moral convictions, which, in turn, are upheld by social support.

For the child, this resonance between parental acting, parental confidence, and social support is a formative experience. It is when the child perceives the parents' acts as truly reflective of their moral and personal stance, and this stance is backed by an interpersonal network, that parental presence is most fully experienced. Children tend to react positively when the parents succeed in manifesting this confluence between acts, values, and support. Even when they protest and put the parents to the test, they may also signal their relief. It is as if they are saying, **"Don't do that!!!** . . . but please, go on!"

Case 1: The Bear Hug*

Miriam managed a supermarket, was a single mother, and the closest friend of her 5-year-old son, Joey. Miriam would come home each day at 4:00 P.M., leaving part of her work to be done in the late evening, after Joey had gone to bed. From the moment she came home until Joey fell asleep, she devoted herself to him. She wanted to compensate him for the lack of a father by giving him as much of herself as she possibly could. She believed in an equal relationship: Joey's opinions should have as much weight

---

*There are two kinds of cases in this book: short vignettes that are untitled and in which the clients remain unnamed, and more detailed cases with titles and fictitious names. In all instances, identifying characteristics have been changed to protect the client's confidentiality.

as her own and everything should be decided by rational argument. Joey, however, often got his way by threatening, by having temper tantrums, and by breaking things, Miriam believed he had learned to be violent from her example, occasions when she lost control and slapped him. She felt guilty for having thus succumbed to anger, thereby traumatizing her son.

Things might have stayed as they were if it were not for some very alarming events. Joey began to do risky things. For example, when the roof of his kindergarten building was being fixed, he climbed to the highest rung of a ladder and threw stones at the children below. He also developed the habit of charging with all his might against the rough outer wall of the kindergarten, bruising himself on the forehead and shoulders. Miriam decided to ask for professional help when she found him asleep on the windowsill with the window wide open. They lived on the third floor.

Miriam felt that she was to blame, that she was bringing Joey up in a state of deep deprivation; in which he not only had to endure her outbursts, but also had to grow up without a father. This deprivation, she said, was why he wanted to destroy himself, and it also explained Joey's anxious behavior. He was so insecure that everything frightened him: dogs, insects, the sea, the dark. He slept in Miriam's bed. He only felt strong when he fought her.

The therapist decided on an immediate home visit. The situation there was far more chaotic than Miriam had described: food debris was everywhere, the walls were covered with scribbling, and the sofa and carpet were badly stained. In the therapist's presence, Joey started kicking a ball against the kitchen cupboard, laughing when the dishes rattled. Miriam followed him, cleaning up and straining to smile at his exuberance. The vibrations in her voice, however, betrayed her anger. She explained to the therapist that Joey was not always like that, and sometimes could be quite reasonable. The therapist asked Miriam to attend another session the next day. The therapist prepared for the session by composing the following message.

You told me that Joey is growing up in a state of deprivation. I think you are right: his alarm signals show that he is under stress. But I do not think that he is deprived of love, attention, or acceptance. I also think that his problems are not necessarily linked to the lack of a father. I believe that Joey may grow up all right without a father, as many children do. Rather, I think that Joey is suffering from rule deprivation and limit deprivation. He needs rules and limits just as much as he needs love and attention. Without these, he cannot grow. I think that when he throws himself against the wall in kindergarten, he is actually asking for a limit. The question is how to set the limits in a nonviolent way. I will propose a procedure that may shock you at first, but which I am sure not only is nonviolent, but is actually antiviolent: in our therapy practice, we call it "the bear hug."

Whenever Joey has a tantrum or starts to scream or throw things at you, pick him up, sit him on your lap, and hug him, strongly. It is best to hold him with his back to you, so that he cannot spit on your face. If he kicks back with his legs, immobilize him with your legs. Don't say a word, as talking will only prolong the struggle. Words are left for other times, when he is not acting violently. He will scream, swear, and struggle. Your job is not to let him get away. You hold him for an hour. He must not know how long it will take. If he asks, don't answer. At the end of the hour, let him go without a word. If he throws a tantrum again, repeat the procedure. You may have to do this a number of times, but I doubt that it will be more than 10.

Now, is this violence? What it clearly is, is power. You are showing yourself to be stronger and in charge. But you are not displaying the essential side of violence: its hit-and-run character, which invariably leaves the victim hurting and abandoned. A child who is beaten or brutally sent away is also getting the message: "I don't want you near!" The contact is minimal: a slap or a kick takes a fraction of a second. Actually, the aim of violence is usually to prevent contact. It is as if the aggressor wants to avoid contamination by the victim's presence. With the bear hug, you are saying the contrary: "I am with you! I don't leave you alone! I am still your mother, even if you scream and curse!" You are also saying, "I can stop you! You cannot frighten me or destroy me!" This is very important, for the world has become a frightening place for Joey. He feels that there is no one there who is stronger than he is, and, therefore, there is no one there to protect him. That's why he is so anxious and afraid. In hit-and-run violence, the victim feels alone and unprotected. With the bear hug, Joey will feel that you are willing to stay with him and by him. After the hug, go back to business as usual. Don't rebuke him or offer him any kind of compensation. But the demands that triggered the clash stay in place.

One more thing. Joey may have a tantrum in a place in which you would feel uncomfortable using the bear hug. If so, wait until you are home and then, briefly reminding him of the tantrum, hug him tightly. And hold him there, in silence, for an entire hour.

Miriam was stunned: she both wanted and feared to try the proposed maneuver. The therapist told her that she could phone any time she wished. After two trials, Miriam called. She said she was worried that Joey was showing signs of despair: 10 minutes after she had started the hug, Joey had gone limp, as if he were dead. Within five more minutes, he had fallen asleep. It seemed to her as if he were losing his will to live. The therapist reassured her, telling her that this probably showed that Joey was feeling secure in her arms. It took some persuasion, but Miriam decided to go on. Altogether, she applied the hug six times. Joey's behavior in kindergarten started to change. He stopped hurting himself and others.

At the end of four weeks, Miriam took Joey to spend a holiday with her family. Miriam's brother was a well-known biologist. Her sister had a Ph.D. degree in psychology and was married to a banker. Miriam had always been viewed as the black sheep of the family. Her status as a single mother was the final confirmation that she was really not on a par with the others. Halfway through the dinner Joey started to behave obnoxiously. Miriam told him to stop and he yelled back at her. She then got up and asked him to come with her to the other room. The parents protested that Miriam was spoiling the family reunion. Miriam answered that she knew best how to bring up her son. She was surprised at the tone of her own voice: she later told the therapist that the event had reminded her of her decision to leave her parents' home at the age of 18, which had made her feel, for the first time in life, worthy and autonomous.

Joey then added the most surprising touch: he went up to Miriam, took her hand in his, and pulled her gently toward the other room: he would side with her against his grandparents, even if they wanted to pamper him. Once in the other room, he sat himself on her lap. Although she hugged him not a whit less strongly, it felt different for both of them. This was the last time the hug was needed. In the coming weeks, Miriam's attitude toward limits changed, with very little coaching from the therapist. She found out, to her surprise, that her skills in running a supermarket were quite helpful in running the home. Joey's anxiety, risk taking, and aggressiveness went down to acceptable levels.

Case 2: The Contract

There was a rumor at school that Peter had said something about wanting to die. No one remembered exactly what he had said, nor did he ever repeat it. However, the danger might be all the more serious for having gone underground. When Peter stopped speaking at home, whatever he might have said at school began to loom larger and larger in his parents' minds. Peter also stopped having his meals with the family. He ate in his room, with his own dishes and cutlery. Lately, he had also started to wash his hands many times a day.

Two years passed without his speaking a word to anyone in his close family. He did not even indicate his needs by gestures. The parents had to guess if he wanted clothes, books, or computer equipment. They got better and better at guessing, simply because when they guessed wrong, the things they bought were left unused and they would have to try again—he did not deign to show them his displeasure. Paradoxically, the less he indicated that he wanted something, the more the parents strove to get things right.

At school, Peter talked, had a few friends, and was a very good student. He also talked to his uncle, to whom he had given, on different occasions, different explanations for his silence: one was that his parents preferred his sister to him; another was that they treated him like a child. Although Peter had never given his parents any special reason for worry until the rumor about his veiled suicide threat at school, his silence, his eating habits, and his hand washing made them fear for his mental balance. They walked as if on eggs, fearing that any mistake on their part might have disastrous consequences.

The family lived in the shadow of Peter's boycott. Guests were only invited in when he was not there, so as not to give let anyone witness Peter's strange behavior. The family had learned to leave him in sole possession of the computer, so as to avoid the silent clashes that inevitably ended with Peter's secluding himself in his room, for hours or days. The parents were too scared to challenge his behavior. Their fears were deepened by two consultations with professionals, who said that Peter needed psychiatric treatment. Since Peter could only be brought to a psychiatrist by force, things stayed as they were. The only changes were that the family socialized less and less, the parents' fears grew, and Peter washed himself more and more frequently.

Mildred and Robert, Peter's parents, consulted a family therapist known for her skill in working with recalcitrant teenagers. She proposed a series of six sessions with the two of them, in which she would attempt to get Peter involved. After the first session with the parents, she sent Peter a letter, informing him that his parents had come to therapy because of their pain at losing him. She had tried to put herself in his shoes and guess at his feelings, but felt it wasn't right for her to try to speak his mind behind his back. The letter ended with an invitation for the coming session: his right to stay silent, if he so chose, would be respected.

The letter, which the parents left on Peter's table, stayed there, seemingly untouched, for a week. However, the night before the session was scheduled, the parents found it, crumpled up, near their bedroom door. The timing showed that Peter had read it. This same sequence was repeated after the therapist's second, third, fourth, and fifth letters. The crumpled page would be punctually delivered the night before each session was to take place. A new ritual seemed to have emerged. At the end of the sixth session, the therapist told the parents there was no point in going on with the same line. She proposed a radical change of direction.

She told the parents that because of their fears, they had become virtually absent from Peter's life. They were afraid to act, speak, and sometimes even think by themselves. Peter probably believed they were fully resigned to never hearing his voice again. Perhaps in his eyes, they did not care enough to put up a fight. The therapist offered to help them to change course and to strive to regain their right to become present in Peter's life. Through the fight they would face their worst fears, instead of cringing before them. They would have to give the treatment full priority and involve at least three additional people from the extended family. The parents asked for time to think about it. Robert, in particular, was very averse to disclosing the secret to other family members.

A few days later, Robert called and said that he had talked to some people in the family. The parents came to the session with four other family members (Peter's uncles and aunts). The following plan was evolved: The parents would take a three-day vacation from work. The night before the program was to be launched, they would search the house for anything with which Peter might hurt himself. They would also remove the keys to the bathroom and all bedrooms. In the early morning, with Peter's uncle already in the house (to help them out if Peter tried to use force or to run away), they would come into Peter's room, wake him up, sit on his bed, and tell him that the situation could not go on as it was and that the boycott on speaking and eating with the family would have to stop. They would have to negotiate and sign a contract (Mildred had thought Peter might take well to the formality of a written agreement), regulating the new state of affairs. They said they would all stay in the house until an agreement was reached.

The parents were told not to expect any quick solution. After waiting a few hours, they were to leave the room and the uncle would step in. His role was to serve as a go-between (this was the uncle to whom Peter talked), making proposals that would enable Peter to start speaking without losing face. He would propose, for instance, that Peter be allowed to begin communicating by gestures or by writing. He would also be allowed to say the first words ("Yes" or "No" answers) with his back to his parents. The uncle, a lawyer, would also help in drafting the actual contract. The other family members would relieve the parents and the uncle in sitting with Peter. Peter was not to be left alone until the agreement was signed and a meal taken in common to seal it. If Peter wanted to go to the bathroom, he would have to indicate his need, if only by a gesture. The parents were instructed not to guess at anything. The therapist would remain on call.

The parents entered Peter's room at 6:00 A.M. For the first four hours, Peter remained silent and sullen. The parents made it clear to him that he would not be allowed to go out and he made no attempt to push them away or to leave by force. The uncle then replaced the parents in the room. After a few minutes of small talk, Peter started to negotiate. As a sop to his dignity, he de-

12

manded a pair of sneakers as a condition for starting to talk with the parents. The parents, after a short consultation with the therapist, decided to agree to the condition: Peter had never before tried any kind of blackmail and if such a tendency became manifest, it could be dealt with in time. For the moment, the goal was to get him to talk and so to allow him any face-saving device he might need. Peter said his first words to his parents at about 2:00 P.M. After another three hours, a complete agreement had been drafted. Then a hitch arose. Peter demanded that his sister not be included in the agreement—with an express written statement to this effect in the contract. The parents denied the condition: they could not agree to legitimize the boycott in any way. Peter reacted by retreating again to total silence. The day's achievements seemed to have gone down the drain.

It took another 24 hours to reach a new compromise. The breakthrough came through the mediation of an aunt who had not been present in the session with the therapist, but who had joined in later on. She lived some distance away and arrived on the scene at 4:00 P.M. on the second day. In contrast to the other family members, she was rested and fresh. Taking Peter aside, she told him that he had absolutely no idea of what he was up against. The parents had stocked up enough food for a three-month siege! She believed, however, that the parents would agree on a compromise about the sister. Peter proposed that he would curtly answer her practical questions and requests (such as to pass him the salt during meals), but he wanted it written in the contract that he had no intention of being her friend. This was deemed acceptable and the agreement was signed. Peter committed himself to answering all questions put to him by saying at least one word. The three aunts and two uncles were present at the signing. Peter's sister (who was at her grandfather's house) was called in for the family meal. Peter had now had 38 hours of the most intensive bout of parental presence he had ever experienced.

In the months that followed, the agreement was kept. Peter did not become talkative (he never had been!), but he replied when spoken to and ate with the family (however, he was allowed his own dishes and cutlery). He also asked for his father's help with math and typed out some material that his mother needed for her work. On a few occasions, he failed to reply to his parents' questions. The witnesses were then called in, the contract was formally read, and Peter agreed to answer the parents, even if only by a single word. In a conversation with his uncle, he said that the contract was very advantageous for him, since it clarified his rights and his real feelings about his sister.

His parents' change in attitude was shown in the following incident. About two months after signing the agreement, Peter refused to budge when his mother asked him to leave his room so that she could clean. Robert intervened and told him peremptorily that, in the past, they had given in to him because they thought he was mentally ill. But now that they knew he was fine, they would not swallow his refusals anymore. Peter backed off. An hour later, he told his mother that he had never thought his father would dare act like that.

Nonetheless, Peter's parents were somewhat disappointed. Although the boycott was over and Peter was on speaking and eating terms with the family, he still kept very much to himself. They had hoped that once he started talking, the dikes would open up. That didn't happen. The changes in the home did not add up to a revolution. However, there was an unexpected improvement: Peter's social life flourished and, for the first time in years, he started to bring friends home. He had evidently been ashamed to invite his pals to his crazy house previously!

Case 3: "I Am Your Mother!"

Anna was 13, the youngest of three adopted children, and very angry. She seemed to have an endless number of complaints against her mother, Rachel: she was always sick, never took her out, never accompanied her to any of the school outings, and had not even given birth to her. What kind of a mother was that? Other parents went camping with their children! Some even played tennis with them! Her mother was a zombie! Why didn't she just drop dead? Who needed her? After raving on and on like this for a while, Anna would slam the door and vanish for hours. To make matters worse, she was fascinated by sex. She talked and read endlessly about sex and was always on the lookout for sexy films on TV. This almost obsessive interest, added to her tendency to disappear, drove Rachel mad with worry.

Anna's outbursts mostly had to do with her mother's illness. Rachel suffered from a congenital heart condition that had prevented her from having children of her own, forced her to rest every few hours, and on occasion required hospital care. In the course of the last year, she had been hospitalized twice and Anna had reacted stormily to both events.

In spite of her physical limitations, Rachel was a very active woman. She worked part-time in a public relations agency (although the family did not need her salary), managed the house, and invested a lot of time in her three children. Moreover, her exceptional social skills helped to compensate for her disability. Thus, she had an important place in the community, known for her ability to organize social events without leaving her room, using no more than her telephone and her powers of persuasion.

Her relationship with her husband, Amos, was very warm. He was gentle, and kind to a fault. Thus, he absolutely refused to be strict with Anna or to set limits on her behavior. His heart melted the moment he saw her. Rachel told the therapist that Amos had dropped out of a previous therapy because the therapist had insisted on his taking a firmer stance with Anna. This was the only area in which he dared to oppose Rachel. In all other respects, he was the perfect husband.

Rachel had once tried, physically, to stop Anna from leaving the house, but the girl had simply pushed her aside. Rachel had begged Amos to back her up, but he had refused, saying that Rachel and the psychologists were wrong. He trusted that Anna would eventually be won over by softness: only love and acceptance could make up for the fact that Rachel and he were not the girl's biological parents.

Anna's outbursts alternated with periods in which she was all sweetness. She would then talk endlessly with Rachel and help her with household tasks. A week might pass in such a honeymoon state. Suddenly, however, Anna would find Rachel in bed or overhear her talking with her doctor and the expected diatribe about her mother's illness would ensue.

When the therapist asked whether Rachel ever succeeded in setting any limits on Anna, she said that she had once disconnected the cable TV and Anna had, surprisingly, held herself in check for two weeks. When she got the TV back, however, the usual troubles returned. Heartened by this successful event, the therapist and Rachel developed a plan that was preceded by the following maternal declaration.

You think that I am not a full person or a full mother because I have a heart condition. You are dead wrong. I never gave up on anything: I never stopped working, I built myself a real family, and I brought up my children without external help. I have never given in to the illness and I am not going to do so!

You are also dead wrong in thinking that I am not a hundred percent your mother. In my acts, in my concern, and in my feelings, I am a hundred percent your mother. You will find out again and again that this is so. You will find it out, even when it will displease you mightily. The fact that I adopted you does not make me any less your mother: on the contrary, I chose to be a mother and decided that you would be my daughter. You can rave as much as you want, but you cannot make me any less your mother.

You think I am weak and you think I cannot cope with you. You will soon see how mistaken you are. I have chosen to be strong, but on my terms. You will find out that I am there also when you are not looking. That I am a mother when you are least thinking about it, when you are busy with other things. You will find out that I am your mother also when you are not at home, when you are at school, when you vanish, and when you are asleep. I am a hundred percent your mother, 24 hours a day, 7 days a week, 4 weeks a month, and 12 months a year. I will be your mother even behind your back. I will be your mother, silently, secretly, and when you least expect.

This message was backed by a series of measures:

1. Whenever Amos was at home and Anna would start raving, Rachel would turn to him and tell him that the noise was disturbing her and that she wanted him to take her out. She knew that Amos would not refuse her: it would be unkind and ungentlemanly.
2. In the wake of an explosion. Anna would find herself unexpectedly deprived of some of her cherished possessions, such as her CDs, her nicest sweater, or even the book she happened to be reading.
3. If Anna came home late or missed school, she would find out that Rachel had been in close contact with the people she knew (many of whom Rachel had skillfully turned into her helpers). This "intelligence net" also allowed Rachel to leave messages for her daughter at various places (e.g., with her tennis coach or friends' parents), some of them intentionally embarrassing.

Rachel found a tingling pleasure in inventing such devices. With the help of her telephone and of her superior persuasion skills, she won the collaboration of many persons with whom Anna was in direct or indirect contact. Anna was, in turn, indignant, mystified, and surprised. Rachel enormously increased her presence in the girl's life. Anna reacted positively. Paradoxically, it was by acting behind Anna's back that Rachel became most present to her and succeeded in showing that she was the hundred percent mother that Anna so desired.

These cases illustrate the parents' recovery of a sense of initiative, personal confidence, and support. These parents dared to experiment with new behaviors undertaken on their own terms, choosing the most fitting time, place, and conditions to make their presence felt. In each case, the therapist strove to make the proposed acts morally and personally acceptable to the parents. In addition, the parents' acts were integrated, as much as possible, within a positive interpersonal context. In all three cases, the parents were enabled to say: "I can act!" "This is right!" "I am not alone!"

The actual steps employed in each case cannot, however, be deduced from the concept of parental presence in itself: there is a conceptual leap between the abstract idea and its concrete implementation. The rest of this book is an attempt to clarify this leap, so as to turn the process into a methodical undertaking that, optimally, can be systematically learned and practiced by therapists and parents alike.

Chapter Two

◆

Parental Presence in the Light
of Other Approaches

(with Uri Weinblatt)

Only one generation ago, the basic assumption shared by most professionals was that there was one true theory and one right treatment for psychological problems. Only one theory could faithfully reflect the *one* real world. This belief is no longer accepted. Perspectives on human behavior are, and always will be, as varied as are the frames of reference of their proponents. These perspectives do not mirror the world in a one-to-one relationship, but reflect our preferred terms of description and angles of observation. This does not mean that the true and the false have become dated: a child was either abused or not abused, ran away from school or didn't run away, tried or did not try to commit suicide. The truth of any of these statements can, in principle, be determined. However, what cannot be resolved with any finality is whether the child was abused, ran away from school, or tried to commit suicide because of unconscious self-destructive urges, ineffective schedules of reinforcement, or inappropriate family boundaries. These explanations reflect different levels of description. Each of them may enrich our understanding, but none describe events at a truer level than do the others. For detailed reviews of this "pluralist revolution" in psychotherapy, see Omer and London, 1988, and Omer and Alon, 1997.

Then why bother about theories? We do because when we talk with professionals, with parents, or even with ourselves, we must frame the conversation in terms of our theoretical concepts, be they explicit or implicit. Thus, when we propose an intervention, we must use our theoretical concepts to justify it. Even our questions come from them, so that in asking whether a child was wanted or not, is withdrawn or expressive, has free access to the parents' room or not, we are, in fact, guided by theory.

However, we cannot assume, as we once did, that our theories represent scientific truth or God's point of view. In particular, we are no longer justified in ruling out *the parents'* perspectives, preferences, or implicit theories. Thus, we no longer can tell them, "This is the right way to think and to act. It is the only one that is enjoined and sanctified by science: if you cannot accept it, so much the worse for you!" In effect, if the parents reject our proposals, it means that the proposals are wrong for these parents or that we did a poor job of explaining them.

In addition, the recognition that different professionals approach the same problems from their own perspectives affects our relationships with these professionals. Indeed, we end up working among a panoply of multiple theories and possible treatments. In the cases we work with, such professionals as educational psychologists, social workers, probation officers, judges, teachers, school principals, physicians, and hospital staff often become involved. Establishing a productive dialogue with these different professionals is of paramount importance. It has been cogently argued that success or failure in difficult cases is more than anything else a function of the ability of the different professionals involved to bridge the gaps between their differences (Elizur & Minuchin, 1993). Thus, when a therapist adopts a position that leaves no room for the opinions of the other professionals involved, the parents and child may suffer. For this reason, there is a pressing need for bridging concepts between different theories. This chapter aims to establish parental presence as such a bridging concept.

A New Behavioral Look at the Mother's Plight

Behavioral therapists have been highly resourceful in devising and validating strategies for helping parents deal with unruly children. The staggering number of studies they have conducted on various disciplinary techniques might, however, blind us to the chief behavioral insight into the process by which mothers become helpless and children tyrannical. This insight is best exemplified by Gerald Patterson's *coercion theory* (Patterson, 1979, 1982).

Patterson hardly fits the stereotype of the behavioral view as one in which the individual is passively molded by external factors. In his rich description, parent and child mold each other: the mother is no less trained by the child than is the child by the mother. Why the mother? Why not both parents? Patterson's answer is empirically grounded: it is simply the mother who bears the brunt of most unpleasant contacts with the child. Thus, the mother is the recipient of 71 percent of all dependent communications (whining and asking for help) and of 56 percent of all aggressive acts (the remaining shares are divided among siblings, the father, and others).

Moreover, while a substantial part of the mother's day is taken up by events that involve friction with the children (in a family with one problem child and one more sibling, a mother can expect to experience more than one unpleasant event per minute!), the father's most common activity (checked by Patterson's careful measuring procedures) is reading the newspaper! To cap it all, when a crisis evolves, the father, more often than not, tends to stay neutral or even to drop out of the scene. Patterson concludes that "the role label most appropriate for fathers might be that of 'guest' " (Patterson, 1980). Even so, Patterson remarks, it would be wrong to conclude that the father does not play an important role: in single-mother families, the amount of friction is even higher than in two-parent families. Patterson's data also show that when the father is more involved, there are fewer problems.

Nevertheless, the heaviest burden falls on the mother. Not surprisingly, studies on maternal mood consistently show a marked decrease in the mother's personal and marital satisfaction during the first 10 years of child rearing (Rollins & Feldman, 1970). For the mothers of aggressive children, the situation is even worse: they have been found to suffer significantly more from anxiety and depression than do the mothers of nonproblem children or those of children with other psychological problems (Anderson, 1969).

This description of the mother's plight sheds light on the cycle of coercion that characterizes the relationship between the mother and the unruly child. Most mothers, as we see, undergo periods of severe strain. If these "normal" troubles are made worse by additional ones (e.g., financial hardship, illness, loneliness, divorce), the mother can be so close to exhaustion that she will be forced to buy some quiet time at almost any price. The stage is then set for the negative mutual training of mother and child.

For instance, say that the mother issues a command. The child often responds by an evasive action or by staging a disturbance. Chances are that if the mother is exhausted, she may back off in order to save energy or end the disturbance. With each repetition of this cycle, the mutual behavior is reinforced: the child's behavior is encouraged by the mother's backing off, and the mother's behavior by the spell of tranquillity she gained. The child will then become more inclined to stage a disturbance, and the mother will become more inclined to back off. Gradually, the child comes to believe that the mother will always back off and the mother will believe that she cannot stand up to the child. Occasionally, the mother may try a firmer stance. The child, more confident of his or her power because of all the previous successes, escalates the unpleasant behavior: whining turns to screaming, screaming to threatening, and threatening to hitting and breaking. Even if the mother holds her own for a while, she is bound to back off eventually. The upshot is that the cycle has been intensified.

Gradually, as higher levels of disturbance are reached, the mother habituates to the lower ones: she may even stop perceiving them. Actually, this is a survival measure: "If you can't control it, don't see it!" This adaptive blindness gradually generalizes to other areas, such as not seeing or knowing with whom the child is socializing and what the child is doing. This maternal selective blindness and paralysis gradually deepens until the mother becomes a virtual absentee from the child's life. If the problem is compounded, as it often is by a marginal or absent father, the child is by this time effectively parentless.

In our opinion, one of the main virtues of this description is that it is very empathic to the mother: she is inexorably led to behave as she does. The outcome is tragic, but no blame is apportioned.

Behavioral programs attempt to counter this cycle by a series of measures:

1. Instructing the parents on the principles of reinforcement (prize and punishment).
2. Training the parents on the observation and measurement of the child's misbehaviors.
3. Defining new reinforcement conditions.
4. Closely monitoring and supporting the parents so that they stick to the program.

These programs aim to redeem the parents from their condition of adaptive blindness and learned helplessness: parents are trained on how to see and how to act. Gradually, as the parents internalize the principles and techniques, they develop their own abilities to initiate action.

Behavioral programs can be quite successful: violence and other disciplinary problems are considerably reduced, maternal self-esteem rises, and the gains can be extended to new settings (such as the school). Lengthy follow-ups show that the changes are often maintained. There are problems, however:

1. considerable dropout rates on the part of the parents;
2. lower success rates with older children, and especially with adolescents; and
3. the reluctance of most professionals to support a strict behavioral stance.

These problems greatly limit the impact of these programs. However, Patterson's insights can be advantageously integrated into a program geared to the establishment of parental presence. As we hope to show, the concept of parental presence offers cogent answers to the issues of parental dropout, professional acceptability, and lower relevance for adolescents.

The Systemic Approach and the Ubiquitous Third Party

Parental presence is a dyadic concept relating to the mutual experiences of parent and child. The chief systemic contribution to our understanding of parental helplessness, however, is precisely to help us look the other way, teaching us to search for a *third party* when trying to understand and influence the parent–child dyad. The typical questions investigated from a systemic perspective are: Which parties enhance or diminish parental presence? Can we stop the leak in parental presence by affecting the third party's relationship to the parent–child dyad? Can we turn negative third parties into positive ones?

For example, in one of the most common *family dances* (a favorite expression of systemic therapists), whenever one of the parents tries to set a limit on the child, the other parent does the opposite and is especially permissive toward the child. The upshot is that the limit-setting parent grows weaker, the child gets stronger, and the marital gap widens. This dance obeys a well-known saying of family therapists: "A child who is taller than one of the parents must be sitting on the other's shoulders."

The third party is not necessarily an individual person. The parent–child dyad is nested in a web of extrafamilial systems that modulate its functioning. Consider the following.

1. *The school.* The relationship between parents and the school can be characterized by either mutual support or sabotage. Everybody knows that the authority of the school is often weakened by parental undermining. The reverse, however, is no less true: parents who fail to collaborate with the teacher or the principal may find their authority curtailed, if only because a major portion of the child's life is now lost from view.
2. *The child's peers.* The influence of peers grows with the child's age, affecting the child's relationship with the parents in greater degrees. In adolescence, the parents' standing may sometimes be virtually at the mercy of the teenager's peer-group judgment.

3. *The community*. The influence of various sectors in the community, such as the church, the police, and the parents' reference group, can be far-reaching. For example, widowed mothers receive far more community support than do divorced or single ones, with predictable results.

4. *The media*. There is hardly an interchange between parent and child that has not been portrayed by the media. Thus, whenever a child threatens, whines, cajoles, or hits; whenever a parent loses control, fights back, or gives in, both parent and child are possessed of images instantiating their ongoing interaction. They have been there already, by proxy, through the mediation of the heroes and heroines of the movies and TV.

Any of these systems can become the focus for a therapeutic intervention. In helping the parents reestablish their presence, the therapist will, at times, find it either opportune or actually necessary to contact the extended family, the school, the child's peers (or the peers' parents), the court, the police, or the church. We cannot, of course, directly influence the media, but in lieu of any program on TV, one can usually find an acceptable one. Sometimes, even the sacrilege of removing the TV set from the child's room or from the house can be committed with amazing results.

Systemic family therapists have perhaps become the staunchest of parental advocates among helping professionals. To many, this may come as a surprise, for family therapy has had very bad press among the general public. Among some segments of the community (particularly with the families of schizophrenics), family therapists have even earned the nickname of "family bashers"! This epithet had some justification with early generations of family therapists, particularly those who made use of pejorative concepts, such as *child scapegoating* and the *schizophrenogenic mother*. However, today this critique is unjust: systemic family therapists have done much to restore parental influence and dignity; to protect abused parents; and to help detect, stop, and reverse the drain on parental presence that is often occasioned by third parties.

The Humanists' Discovery of the Parent as a Person

We refer to humanists as professionals who view the client as a person possessed of a unique self and who relate to him or her as the center of all therapeutic activity. But is this not a truism? Do not all therapists subscribe to this belief? That is, undoubtedly, the official credo. However, by an ironic twist in the history of the helping professions, parents have often been all but deprived of their right to be viewed as individuals. The reason is simple: the child comes first. In our culture, when parents and children are considered together, the fuller rights are assumed to be the child's. With the helping professions, this preference rests on a theoretical judgment, as well as on a value judgment: all psychological problems stem from the privations and deprivations of childhood.

Thus, in setting the child's interest at the center, we shall be caring not only for the child's immediate well-being, but also for the future mental health of society. Parents should understand that this is their responsibility. Their individual interests and needs must be subordinated to those of the child. Moreover, since the parents are to be held responsible for the ills of the child, it is only fitting that they should bear the burden of reparation.

Although these positions are seldom made explicit, their influence is undeniable. Until quite recently, for instance, little was written or said about parents as victims of children's aggression. Ill treatment was assumed to be unidirectional: it made sense to speak only of children as victims. When we told people that we were conducting clinical research concerning parents who are abused by their children, they responded with a puzzled look ("Are there such cases?") or, misunderstanding this altogether, they encouraged, us in our efforts against the plague of child abuse. This selective blindness is so pronounced that it took the daring of pioneers to unmask the facts about parental victimization and to raise the claim that parents should be viewed as individuals in their own right.

One of the original voices in this respect was that of Donald Winnicott, who argued that a parent's very human flaws are essential to a child's development. Indeed, if the mother were perfectly attuned to the child's needs, the child would not thrive. Fortunately, Winnicott remarks, the mother's "petty" individual needs guarantee that the ideal attunement shall be appropriately blemished (Winnicott, 1965).

Winnicott speaks very strongly where aggression is concerned: the child's violence must be opposed fully and emotionally, or the child will not feel that other people are really alive. Unless the child's anger is met by real anger, he or she may suspect that the other's love is also not fully real (Winnicott, 1958). To remove any doubts that Winnicott's meaning is far from metaphorical, we have only to quote his own reaction to the maddening behavior of a parentless boy of 9 whom he took into his house during the war.

> *Did I hit him? The answer is No, I never hit. But I should have had to have done so if I had not known all about my hate and if I had not let him know about it too. At crises I would take him by bodily strength . . . and put him outside the front door, whatever the weather or the time of day or night. . . . Each time, just as I put him outside the door . . . I said that what had happened had made me hate him. This was easy, because it was so true.* (Winnicott, 1958, p. 200)

Winnicott goes on to say that the boy's deeply rooted relationship to the Winnicott family remained one of the few stable things in his life. We believe that this was so because Winnicott had made himself present to the boy in all of his human feelings and failings; even bitter hatred was not skipped or prettified.

Such unencumbered expressions of hate cannot, of course, be displayed to a baby or a small child. Containing one's own anger is one of the vital challenges of early parenthood. However, Winnicott argues that some roundabout satisfaction of motherly anger is obtained by hallowed cultural means, such as the sadistic lullaby: "Rockabye baby, on the tree top/When the wind blows, the cradle will rock/When the bough breaks, the cradle will fall/ Down will come baby, cradle and all." With time, however, the child becomes more capable of being faced with true angry responses. The "ideal" parent who succeeds all too well in the task of self-control will then be depriving the child of a vital developmental experience. If this is to happen, Winnicott adds, the child will remain infantilized.

Another parental feeling that has been recently rehabilitated by psychoanalytic writers, after having been long proscribed, is the parental wishful fantasy. In the past, it was often assumed that such fantasies expressed narcissistic needs that would warp the child's growth. Today, however, parental fantasies are not only being allowed again, but even recommended (Elson, 1984)! Of course, a measure of flexibility is needed. Consider, for example, the following contrasting stories (Elson, 1984, p. 303).

The first story is about the father of Richard Strauss, who was himself a distinguished horn player. In a letter to his son, concerning a performance of the latter's tone poem *Macbeth*, the father urged him: "I counsel you, although heavy hearted because I know it is useless, to revise Macbeth . . . and give the *horns* more opportunity to stand out."

The second story is about Eugene Ormandy's father, who used

to force his son to practice on the violin by repeated beatings whenever he stopped playing. In later years, the father was invited by the grown-up Eugene (who had long since abandoned the violin) to a violin concert that he conducted. After the concert, the father commented, "If only I had beat you more, *you* would have been playing the violin and *he* would have been conducting!"

Both fathers had no dearth of wishful fantasies about their sons. Both were hurt by their dreams not having been realized according to blueprint. Strauss's father, however, reacted by expressing a poignant wish to have Richard infuse a bit more of his own fatherly self (the horns) into his tone poem; Ormandy's father responded by a show of rejection quite fitting with his earlier cruel methods. We would, of course, recommend Papa Strauss's flexible narcissism rather than Papa Ormandy's rigidity.

Evidently, some children suffer from the rigid ambitious fantasies of their parents. However, might not others suffer no less from the lack of such fantasies? In the families we are discussing, the answer is an unqualified "Yes." Helpless parents are usually so hopeless that they cannot entertain in earnest even the mildest of expectations about their children. It is as if they view hope as a dangerous virus: hoping means trying, trying means demanding, and demanding means failing amid an uproar of mutual grievances. We have, however, heard many a belated complaint by these children against their parents: "You never believed I might amount to something!"

It would be no exaggeration to say that the parent as an individual has been "discovered" by professionals only recently. Talking about parents in and of themselves seemed so counterintuitive that one of the pioneering books about parents as human beings begins with an apology: "Although we love children dearly, not much will be said about children—the libraries are full of books about them" (LeMasters & DeFrain, 1989, p. 3).

The "discovery" of the parent started with the understanding that he or she has often been judged unfairly and unrealistically. Thus, parents have been deemed responsible for anything that goes wrong with their children. Mothers, especially, have been blamed for making their children hyperactive, schizophrenic, or transsexual (Caplan, 1986).

Additionally, parents have had to submit not only to judgment by their peers (other parents), as is usually the case in the evaluation of other roles, but also to that of therapists, teachers, physicians, nurses, and judges. Furthermore, these demands coincide with a historical period of decreasing support by the extended family. To cap it all, although they are submitted to growing demands and judged by harsher criteria, the parents who dare to ask for external help are viewed with a critical eye, perhaps more than ever.

The new sympathetic outlook on parents has been followed by the shattering of myths. For instance, the belief that "in the old days" parents were less abusive, and, on the whole, more successful, has been cogently contested by research (LeMasters & DeFrain, 1989; Straus & Gelles, 1986). Also, the "empty-nest syndrome" seems to be rather uncommon: research consistently reveals that marital and personal satisfaction decrease after the birth of babies but rise once again as the children become more independent. The peak, however, is reached when the children leave the home! When the "empty nest" is filled again because a child returns home after failing to live on his or her own, parental satisfaction sinks to its lowest level (Glenn & McLanahan, 1982; White, Booth, & Edwards, 1986).

Books, courses, and support groups for parents focus more and more on the rights of parents as human beings and on the distortions that an exclusively child-centered perspective has brought to family life. New metaphors and parables are being fashioned in the service of a new balance. In one of these, the home should no longer be viewed as a circle with a unique center—the child—

but as an ellipse with two centers—the parent and the child. A tale typical of this new spirit tells of a mother who, coming back from the market, is set upon by her children, screaming for food. She closets herself in the kitchen and fixes herself a good meal. When asked how she can be so selfish, she replies: "I am preparing a strong and healthy mother for them!" (Amit, 1997).

Of all parent-affirming voices, however, none can compete in emotional impact with that of self-help groups like "Parents Anonymous" and "Toughlove." Joining such a group often has the immediate effect of releasing the parents from the wheel of blame and guilt to which they are shackled. Parents suddenly find out that their pains and difficulties are not shamefully unique. They learn that they deserve the luxury of a livable home, that they are entitled to some respite from continuous struggle, and that their personal voices can and should be heard. They also get the opportunity to receive and give actual support, without which sympathy can be but meager fare. These groups have helped many parents to gain back their almost obliterated sense of moral and personal value.

Parental Presence as an Integrative Approach

The behavioral, systemic, and humanist perspectives have mapped three pathways to parental absence:

1. Behavior therapists describe the progressive loss of the parents' capacity for action. The child, in contrast, grows ever more confident in his or her power to rule by disturbances.
2. Systemic thinkers underscore the draining of parental presence by extraneous factors. The child, in turn, learns to count on these factors to neutralize the parents.

3. Humanists focus on the parents' loss of their personal voices. The child responds by viewing them as hollow figureheads.

The parental presence approach is an attempt to integrate these different insights, both conceptually and practically. Conceptually, instead of viewing the behavioral, systemic, and humanistic perspectives as mutually exclusive, we can see them through the unifying prism of parental presence as complementary. Practically, our triple goal is to help the parents become fully present by: (a) regaining the capacity to act, (b) putting a stop to systemic leaks, and (c) recovering their personal voices. We can assume these efforts to be synergistic.

This triple goal can be also formulated from the child's perspective. Our aim is, thus, to rescue the child from: (a) a vacuum of parental guidance and protection, (b) a chaos of mutually disqualifying influences, and (c) a lack of an individualized parental figure. The following three chapters take up each of these facets of parental presence.

Chapter Three

◆

Behavioral Presence

Parent become paralyzed by fear, by pity, by too much speaking or too much listening, by believing too much in specialists or too little in themselves. In this chapter, we explore ways of tracing and reversing these processes. Our goal is to get parents back into action, even parents that therapists view as "unmotivated," "not up to the task," or "unfit for parenting." Actually, these negative characterizations of parents are more reflective of our helplessness as therapists rather than the parents' true condition. In no small degree, we therapists are responsible for our own negative views. Correcting them and evolving an attitude of respect for parents may well be the first crucial step in the treatment.

Respect for Parents

As we discussed in the previous chapter, the helping professions were long blind to seeing parents as human beings, and as individuals in their own right. To correct this bias, we must not only acknowledge it, but also find new ways of thinking about and speaking to parents; in other words, respecting parents and expressing our respect.

First and foremost, therapeutic respect should be expressed with regard to parents' pain, values, and achievements. Respecting parents' pain means showing our recognition that the fears and hurts they suffer from or because of their children are legitimate and important. This seemingly trivial rule is often left in abeyance. Thus, a common reaction to the complaints of parents is, "They must have done something to deserve it." This response is totally unacceptable when working with any and all abused people. Luckily, where other victims are concerned, such as battered or raped women and especially abused children, there is a growing awareness of the damage caused by this blaming attitude. Unfortunately, parents have benefited less from this positive trend: somehow their pain is deemed to be less defensible than the pain of other types of victims. Therefore, parents are often very surprised when a therapist shows a real interest in their hurts, refuses to accept that they are to blame, and offers to help them protect themselves.

We therapists are also guilty of showing disrespect for parents' values. Thus, we often speak of parents as too achievement-oriented, as caring too much for their own needs and fantasies, or as holding a narrow view of child rearing. Sometimes, we even succumb to the temptation to teach them how to parent by showing them how *we* deal with the child in the session. For example, some play therapists invite parents to be passive observers in their sessions with the child, so as to show them how one can be truly warm and empathic. Similarly, some discipline-oriented therapists try to show the parents how best to deal with the child at home by the way they put a stop to the child's disturbance in the session. Although these examples may be too obvious, we all fall prey to more subtle forms of these same mistakes.

The third facet of respect is in regard to the parents' achievements. Much has been said about the bias of therapists for the negative and the pathological. Indeed, we often see parents through the lens of their failures, overlooking the fact that a child who is obstreperous at home may be doing well at school or that the parents may have been successful with other children in the family. It cannot be overemphasized that the salutary contrary attitude of highlighting successful experiences can be deeply meaningful for the parents and extremely useful for the therapy.

When we look at these three kinds of disrespect, it becomes clear how we often come to see the parents as incapable and unmotivated. No wonder, since we have actually done our best to view them as such!

However, a question imposes itself: how are we to help the parents change, if we keep confirming them in their positions? Our answer is that we can best challenge the parents' ineffective patterns and help them to change them, if they feel cogently confirmed by us in their pain, in their values, and in their achievements. Challenge and support are thus the two sides of the same coin: the more forceful our empathic endorsement of the parents' pain, values, and achievements, the greater our ability to contest their ineffective behavior.

The therapeutic messages in this book will almost always take this dialectical form, beginning with a cogent empathic expression of respect and closing with an equally strong challenge (Omer & Alon, 1997; Omer, 1998). The two parts of the message reinforce each other: the challenge is all the more acceptable because of the preceding empathic support and the support is all the more credible because of the ensuing challenge. In a way, this support–challenge attitude in the therapeutic sphere reflects the message of parental presence. Thus, the parent will be saying to the child, "I am with you; therefore, I can prevent you from acting destructively!" Likewise, the therapist can say to the parents, "I am with you and respect your pain, values, and achievements; therefore, I can help you change your acts!"

Bodily Presence

The earliest and most basic way by which the parents become present to the child is through the body. The parent is there by holding, hugging, and handling the baby. With growth, bodily presence becomes more intermittent and new, symbolic ways of manifesting parental presence become available. The need for bodily presence, however, does not vanish: when the child starts to move around, climb a ladder, or use a swing, the parent's protective and restraining hands play a vital role. In all of these activities, the very difference in size between parent and child can be deeply meaningful. For example, when the child cries uncontrollably, it is within the parent's capacious embrace that the crying and the screaming gradually subside.

In effect, at least for a small child, all emotional outbursts may find their harbor in the big arms of Mother or Father. In some respects, this emotional "use" of the parents' (or of another loved one's) arms continues throughout life. However, we tend to think that as the child grows, one may still make good use of the embrace that comforts, but not of the one that restrains. But can we be sure that the two are very different after all? The first case example (see Chapter 1, "The Bear Hug") argues against any such clear-cut distinction.

The body is our touchstone of reality. Thus, we pinch ourselves to confirm that we are not dreaming. For a child whose parents have become virtually absent, we can surmise that the renewed experience of the parents' bodily presence will become the most cogent reminder of their existence. If the parents' bodies are there, thick and unshakable, the child is not dreaming after all! When children react with skepticism to the parents' initial attempts to come back to the family stage, nothing silences their doubts as well as the parents being physically there.

To a small child, few things can compare with the bear hug as immediate proof of a parent's unshakable presence. We have used it in dozens of cases involving tantrums and violent outbursts. Most of the children were under age 10. Although I usually suggest that the bear hug last for an hour, many parents make spontaneous discounts on this period of time without any remarkable loss in effectiveness—unless they shorten it to a few hesitant and guilty minutes. Most parents are willing to implement the bear hug once the therapist takes the trouble to explain what messages are conveyed by it: "I am here!" "I won't leave you!" "I won't give up!" "I am stronger than you!" "I can withstand your anger and your hurt!" "I will stay with you for as long as it takes!" Parents understand full well the enormous difference in the messages given in the bear hug than those conveyed, let's say, by a slap. Although this procedure was highly effective in almost all of our cases, I would like to describe an instructive failure:

> *Violent 9-year-old twins developed a peculiar reaction to the parents' attempts to apply the bear hug: whenever one of them was being held, the other would ask why he or she was not! Alternatively, when both were held, each twin would complain that he or she was being held more painfully. The parents would then try to equalize the conditions, which only led to further complaints. After a few attempts, the parents gave up on the strategy.*

Territory

With older children, direct contact as conveyed by the bear hug may be replaced by steps dealing with freedom of movement and personal space. Thus, when a teenager flouts a parent's prohibition against leaving the house at an inappropriate hour, the parent may block the exit with his or her body. The message—"I am here, I won't give up, and I won't budge!"—is far stronger than one conveyed by words alone. The impact is all the greater if the parent remains by the door for a very long time, many hours if possible, almost like a mythological guardian. In one case, after a stormy scene, a teenager woke up at 3:00 A.M., only to find his father still at his post.

But what if the teenager succeeds in evading the parental guard? Has the measure been invalidated? Not necessarily! The very fact that evasion is needed signifies some degree of parental presence (in contrast to the teenager who assumes that the parent will do nothing). Moreover, the parent can pursue the territorial dialogue by setting up a search for the fugitive and arriving, in person, at places that are taboo for parents. Thus, we have encouraged our clients to make surprise visits to street corners, video arcades, drug hangouts, and clubs. The appearance of a couple of middle-aged parents at a club, searching for their daughter and asking everybody if they know her or saw her, can be a rather "constructive trauma."

The impact of these interventions is derived from the deep-seated territoriality of our species. From very early on children care deeply for the physical trappings of their privacy: "This is *my* toy, *my* bowl, *my* bed, my room!" Parents tend to honor these claims, even while trying to teach the child to respect the claims of others and to evolve a readiness to share. Indeed, possession and territory are important keys to the development of individuality.

But territory is not only a function of one's power, it is also a major source of power. Thus, all territorial animals fight most fiercely when closest to the heart of their territory. Many adolescents behave as if this were true for them: when the sacredness of their territory is at stake, they may fight with a fury of which they are not capable elsewhere. In one of our cases, a 15-year-old boy, who had never been physically violent to his mother, reacted to her entering his room without knocking by flinging her out, girdling her throat with his fingers, and threatening to kill her if she ever did it again. There is also a report of a teenager who trained a hound to attack anyone who dared enter his room in his absence (Icami Tiba, 1996). Some adolescents actually barricade themselves in their rooms, leaving them only at night for plundering expeditions throughout the house. In many such cases, I would venture that contesting the child's absolute territorial claims often proves to be a turning point in the treatment.

> The mother of a 7-year-old girl asked for help because of a series of impositions that her daughter inflicted on her: every night, the locks of all doors and windows in the house had to be thoroughly inspected by the girl and her mother. The mother then had to turn all the dolls in the girl's room with their eyes to the wall, to the accompaniment of a highly ritualized good night routine.
>
> The therapist proposed a counterritual: the mother should take the girl through all the rooms of the house, naming the different objects and saying to her daughter (and to herself) that they all belonged to the parents. For each item, she should specify when it was bought and how much it had cost. The ritual was to be concluded with the statement:
>
> "This house and everything in it belongs to me and Daddy. Your room belongs to us because we bought it and paid for it. All the doors and windows belong to us. Even your dolls are actually our guests and they have to abide by the rules of the house. Of course, this is your home, because you are our daughter. But we own everything. From now on, we take care of locking the house and will not accept another word from you. Furthermore, in our house no dolls sleep with their eyes to the wall. If, in the morning, we find them in that position, they will spend a week in our closet. Good night."
>
> The intervention had an immediate impact. The nightly rituals disappeared and were not replaced by new ones. The girl also became calmer during the day. It is as if she had previously felt

that she was alone in the big house, but now the parents had come back.

One basic territorial intervention that is especially useful with adolescents is the *sit-in*: the parents enter the child's room and stay in it for hours on end, if need be, day after day. The youngster is prevented from leaving or from throwing them out. Little talking is necessary: all I recommend to the parents is to say that things cannot stay as they are. The goal is to bring the child to negotiate, *seriously*. The sit-in is actually a versatile intervention, with many other uses besides the territorial one (Also see, "The Contract" (Chapter 1), and "Treating the Wild Dozen through Self-Prescribed Reparations," (Chapter 5).

Children can carve out for themselves other kinds of personal space, besides their actual room. For example, many parents would agree that the children's money should be their own to use as they see fit, and usually the parent-child experience is positive when the child is allowed this freedom. On occasion, however, the child's freedom may paralyze the parents in vital areas. In one of our cases, the parents of a diabetic boy felt unjustified in limiting the boy's use of his own funds to buy mountains of sweets, which repeatedly put him into a state of hyperglycemia.

I propose that parents follow the rule that the personal space of children should be respected, but only to the extent that it is put to legitimate use. However, when territorial immunity becomes the mainspring of the child's destructive power, nothing will help, unless the parents are willing to wage an all-out battle over it.

The Time Factor

A scene from a film: a boy is peremptorily told not to leave the table before finishing his food. The camera then shows him sitting alone by the untouched dish, with the passage of time intimated by changes in lighting. After what seems like a very long interval, the father comes in and tells the child to go to his room. Although such situations surely happen, it is unusual for a child of any age to hold his or her own in a carefully planned battle of endurance decreed by the parents. The tactical disciplinary victory is only a small fraction of the real aim: to convey, by means of the parents' staying power, the incontrovertible message of their presence. The time factor plus the territorial one actually make up the *cogito* of parental presence: "I take up time and space, therefore I am!"

However, control over the time factor goes beyond patience and endurance. The question of initiative is also highly important. Parents who merely react to the child's moves often seem deprived of a will of their own. In contrast, the recovery of initiative restores them to the status of autonomous beings. In the case "I Am Your Mother!" (Chapter 1), the mother's readiness to act on her own terms, rather than merely reacting to her daughter's provocation, transformed her from an invalid absentee into someone to be reckoned with. She had become unpredictable! In effect, this is a very good way to become present in someone's mind, for our nervous system reacts most strongly to the unusual and the unexpected. Constructive unpredictability, however, should be planned well in advance!

The parents of two boys (ages 7 and 9) complained that their children turned every family outing into an ordeal by their endless screaming and fighting. The father would often stop the car and threaten that he would never take them out again. The boys would then stay quiet for a while but start rioting again once the ride was resumed. At the therapist's suggestion, the parents told the children that they would all go canoeing. The boys put on their swim suits ahead of time, so as not to lose time on arriving. As the car reached the highway, which to the boys signified "holiday," they started yelling. The father told the

mother that he didn't feel like canoeing anymore and she agreed;
they made a U-turn and returned home. This positive trauma
was reinforced by another two months later.

Children's freedom of initiative relative to their parents' is often shown in the timing of their disturbances. Thus, children feel much more at ease in putting their parents to shame than the opposite. There are, of course, good cultural reasons why this is so: after all, it is usually parents who teach children the rules of decorum. Still, when children not only feel free to embarrass their parents, but carefully pick the very situations where their parents are most fearful to create a scene in which they press their demands, a battle for "the right to embarrass" may be in order.

A woman who conducted weight-control groups had been re-
peatedly pressured by her daughter into writing false letters to
the teacher, saying that she (the girl) had not done her home-
work because of a migraine. On one occasion, when the mother
refused to give in, the girl typed the letter and brought it to the
mother to sign in the middle of a group session. Fearing a scene,
the mother signed the letter without a word. But the next morn-
ing when the girl delivered the letter, the teacher told her that
the mother had called, saying that the letter had been coerced
from her and that the daughter never suffered from migraines.

Case 4: The Sit-in

Amy had started to withdraw at the age of 17. She stopped eating with the family, talking to her parents (Jean and Ben), and meeting with friends. Her daily schedule became limited to an English course she was taking, part-time work in a library, a bus trip to work and back, and endless hours in her room. She also became spiritual (for a few months).

She developed peculiar eating habits. Sometimes, for a whole day, she would eat only bean sprouts and drink mineral water. Jean feared she was becoming anorectic. Since Amy ate only when her mother was not there, Jean always left the kitchen the moment Amy opened the door of her room, hoping that this would increase the chances that Amy might eat. After eating, Amy would throw the garbage out of the window. She soon starting throwing other things as well—even her underwear, stained with menstrual blood.

During the night, Amy would sometimes leave her lair and go on plundering expeditions throughout the house. Jean started to miss articles of clothing. A watch and a bracelet also disappeared. When Amy was at work, Jean searched her room, and found the missing articles. When Jean confronted Amy with her find, Amy made a dismissive gesture and closeted herself in her room. Jean and Ben consulted a psychiatrist, who said Amy was probably schizophrenic.

The parents consulted with a family therapist when Amy, now 20, gave up her job, as well. She had become a total recluse. With the therapist's encouragement, Jean dared to make her first tentative steps in regaining some of the lost territory. Thus, she no longer left the kitchen when Amy opened her door. Amy adapted herself to the new situation, eating when Jean was away. Jean and Ben were encouraged by this small change.

In the course of the sessions, some new facts were brought to light: Amy had always been finicky about her personal belongings. From a very early age, nobody was allowed to touch her things. She would spend hours arranging her room and would become enraged if something were out of place. As she grew up, these traits became more and more pronounced. Even her gestures gave the impression that all was smoothly under control. The emerging picture was different from the one suggested by the psychiatrist: Amy seemed to be obsessive-compulsive. Jean and Ben reacted well to this new, more hopeful, label. The therapist told them that the best way to check this would be to challenge Amy in her own territory: if she suffered from obsessive-compulsive disorder, she might react positively after a strong initial bout of anxiety. Jean and Ben were willing to try.

The therapist instructed Jean and Ben to enter Amy's room together and stay there for three hours at a time. Jean might clean the room, meanwhile (Amy had long given up her orderly habits and her room was now a total mess). If Amy became violent, Ben should restrain her from hitting them. The therapist would be on call around the clock. The goal was to challenge Amy's unquestioned territorial immunity and to bring her to the point of negotiating.

The reaction was unbelievably quick. Ben's scratched cheek and Jean's black eye were the only battle casualties. When Ben restrained her, Amy started to scream. She screamed for an hour. She then started to whine, which she did for the duration of two additional sit-ins. By the end of the third sit-in, Amy started to talk. At first she tried to set up a coalition with Ben, at Jean's expense. When this failed, she decided to negotiate. No further sit-ins were necessary. Amy went back to eating with the family. After a week, she went shopping with her mother (she had not done so since the age of 15). She went back to work part-time and decided to attend the university. She has been studying successfully for the last two years and has not closed herself off again.

Information and Supervision

As the child grows, the parents' presence becomes manifest in new ways. Now, instead of being there physically most of the time, the parents show their presence and assert their care by knowing of the child's whereabouts and doings and by the child knowing that they know. With time, both child and parents have to be weaned from this supervision. However, the big question is how fast and to what extent.

Privacy is a major cultural value in the West. Privacy needs grow as the child grows, and the continuous frustration of privacy may disturb the child's development. Children with acute behavioral problems suffer most from a lack, rather than an excess, of parental supervision (Chamberlain & Patterson, 1995). The parents, however, may find it difficult to institute the required supervision precisely because of the high value in which privacy is held in the culture. Although many teenagers are known to be involved in troublesome activities, they can get their parents off their backs simply by telling them of the greater degree of privacy allowed to their peers. Many parents do not even need this reminder: they limit their supervision spontaneously—out of respect for the sacredness of privacy. Modifying this self-effacing stance is a considerable step for many parents. It helps to tell them that research shows that parental supervision reduces the risk of drugs and delinquency (Kolvin, Miller, Fleeting, & Kolvin, 1988).

> *A teenager, who was becoming involved with a street gang, paralyzed his parents by threatening to run away from home if they meddled with his affairs. In the first therapeutic interview, the parents reached the conclusion that their policy of nonintervention was only making matters worse. The father decided he would start shadowing the boy and getting all information he could about him. He spent three weeks making phone calls and following the boy closely. After one week, the boy told his mother that the father was quite a detective. This shadowing activity gave the boy a good excuse for reducing his involvement with the gang: after all, he did not want to become an unwitting informer! One might surmise that under the new conditions, the gang was also happy to see him go.*

As with the other authority measures proposed above, the goal of parental supervision is not merely control, but the conveyance of presence. Sometimes, the news unearthed by parental research is that their child is not doing such bad things, after all. In one of our cases, the boy's secret doings turned out to be quite positive! Whatever its results, however, the message conveyed by the supervision is not only "Big Daddy is watching you!" but also "We are close by! We have not despaired!"

Words

One of the child's escape valves that is notorious for draining parental presence is the parents' endless talking. Helpless parents continuously threaten, explain, exhort, entreat, blame, and apologize. This talking becomes a background drone that makes the parents count for less and less in the child's eyes and also in their own. Actually, the talking convinces not only the child, but also the parents, that no action will be taken. The question is how to stop the droning and help the parents speak less, but with words that have meaning.

It sometimes helps to point out how badly the talking hurts their standing. When asked if the child ever tries to draw them into arguments so as to prevent their taking action, they often smile. Many parents know that the child ridicules their admonishments. Some teenagers, for example, are masters in the art of caricaturing the parents' speaking style. The value of parental words can be gradually renewed by silence, unusual acts, and the judicious use of new ways of communicating. These processes reinforce each other.

The mother of an abusive teenager described how she decided to stop all her services to her son after he threw her out of his room in the presence of his friends. What surprised her most in her own behavior was that she stopped talking for the duration of her strike, without deciding about it beforehand. She felt that

the silence hardened her resolve. When communication was re-
sumed, it was different for both.

The silence retreat, particularly if accompanied by other steps
that restore parental presence, can be a powerful measure. It
might seem that silence, being a form of disconnection, is opposed
to the principle of parental presence. This is not so, however: it
is the endless verbal flow that signifies absence since the words
have come to mean nothing. Silence may then carry the meaning
that the parent is back!

If this might seem somewhat puzzling, consider the following
well-known phenomenon: whenever a person is subjected to a
constant physical stimulus, he or she not only stops reacting to
it, but also stops consciously perceiving it. The stimulus even
ceases to arouse any manifest neural response. This phenomenon
is called *habituation*. However, the moment the constant stimulus
is withdrawn, the brain (and the person) react. Silence has thus
been turned into signal! The same is true of the parents' incessant
talking. Its interruption may cause the child to perceive the parents as being there.

New acts can lend life to the parent's words but, sometimes,
the old words grew stronger and invalidate even the most decided
steps. For example, a parent who undertakes the bear hug while,
at the same time, explaining, exhorting, and apologizing, weakens
the hug: the "old" parent that comes through in the verbal flow
all but effaces the perception of the "new" and present parent.

Words can also be brought to life by being expressed in new
contexts or modalities, as in the following example.

An adolescent girl, whose parents had divorced, refused to see
her father or to talk to him on the phone. The therapist per-
suaded the father to write her a letter every week. He was to
set himself a fixed weekly hour for the task and persevere with
it, regardless of the girl's response. The therapist warned him

that it might take a very long time, months or even years, until he got a response. The father kept a copy of each letter he sent. The girl tore up the first few letters.

After a month, however, she stopped tearing them up, leaving them, instead, unopened on the shelf. One year later, during a time when she was having bad fights with her mother, she started to read them. It took her yet another year to start meeting with her father. She then told him that the letters had been a source of great comfort for her. She said that even before she had started reading them, their regular arrival and mere physical presence on the shelf served as cogent witnesses to his enduring care.

Whenever I give parents a writing assignment, I try to help them keep their letters as free as possible from the negative elements that contaminate their face-to-face communication with the child. Exhortations, threats, accusations, entreaties, and apologies should be carefully avoided. We often peruse the letters in the sessions, so as to sensitize them to these elements. Gradually, they learn to write as individuals, relating their daily events, concerns, and plans for the future. Some parents write about earlier times with the child or about their own childhoods. Some enrich the letters with photographs. One father told me that his writing did much to improve his conversations with his child.

Fear

To bring parents out of their helplessness, it is crucial to address their fears. Parents are in the peculiar position of having to fear both for their own side (that the child may attack or reject them) and for the child's side (that they may cause pain and damage or push the child to dangerous extremities). This double front can be profoundly debilitating. However, all therapeutic efforts will remain shaky, unless the parents get some feeling of influence over their most dreaded outcomes. Therefore, parental fears must be set squarely at the center of the therapeutic dialogue. It may then be possible to channel these fears in the therapy's favor. How? The first step is to make them explicit. Therapists should ask the parents for their most frightening scripts: their worst thoughts should be given their worst words.

One should assume that the parents' fears are never trivial. Those that seem so are often only a screen for more ominous ones. In the parents' minds lurk lurid cases that give substance to their catastrophic scripts. The therapist should take pains to un-earth them. Not that their mere spelling out has the power to dissipate them, as sometimes happens with other anxious clients. Fears about children tend to be more tenacious than fears for the self. The prospect of a child's being sent to a mental hospital, becoming addicted to drugs, or committing suicide clings malig-nantly to the mind. The summoning up of the parents' fears must, therefore, be a preamble to the parents' mobilization to a pro-gram of action based on parental presence.

Once the most awful fears are made explicit, we reach what is perhaps the focal point of the whole therapy: therapist and par-ents then turn their attention to the very point of parental sur-render. Indeed, it is the parents' fears that force them to give in, even to the most unacceptable demands and behaviors. Viewed in this light, the parents' behavior is perfectly understandable. What might have been seen as indicating parental spinelessness now comes to light as parental concern. The parents stand ab-solved. The stage is set for a shift to the positive.

The therapist should discuss with the parents why giving in at these moments is probably the most dangerous option. Giving in carries a message of despair. It is tantamount to parental abdi-cation. The child cannot but feel abandoned at the height of the storm. What is most needed, by parents and child alike, is a clear manifestation of parental presence: not to give in, not to hit and run, and not to let go, but to remain by the child in body and mind and to act in ways that say: "We are here!" "We won't give you up!" "We can't be shaken off!"

The parents should know that the operation may take months. The therapist should ask them whether they are willing to give first priority to the task. The goal, however, should be stated in very clear and positive terms: to turn their absence into presence, so as to become a real, positive factor in their child's life.

The more extreme the parents' fears, the greater the impact and the mobilizing power of this message. This is clearest when the fear of the child's committing suicide haunts the parents' every thought, from the moment they get up in the morning to the last of their sleepless hours at night. The work of parental presence is then the only way not to leave the child in a vacuum and not to convey a message of despair. Parents view the child who threatens or attempts suicide as living at the brink. If so, their best course is to struggle for their right to remain present, so as not to leave the child alone at that brink. There is hope in this struggle: the parent who stays present may be close enough to prevent the jump. Furthermore, by staying there, the parent helps the child to feel less alone and hopeless.

However, many parents fear that the very fight for presence may give the extra push to send the child over. But suicide is an act of loneliness and despair, and the conveyance of decided care is a strong antisuicidal measure. It is the giving in and being left alone that, in the long run, kill. Parents understand this well. The therapeutic endeavor that is launched on this key may never suffer from lack of motivation.

Case 5: Overcoming Fear and Estrangement

Shelly had been adopted at birth. She came from another continent and looked very different from her parents. In her first year of life, she was sickly and suffered innumerable illnesses. Sam and Ruth had repeatedly had to take her to the hospital. However, when she started to walk, she suddenly became exceptionally healthy, strong, and beautiful. It was as if she had undergone a sort of biological adaptation to her new surroundings.

Each transition, however, exacted a heavy price. It took months for her to adapt to kindergarten and the passage to elementary school was even worse. Although she was highly intelligent and no learning disabilities were diagnosed, Shelly found all school subjects extremely hard. The school psychologist was at a loss to explain her abysmal difficulties. This reinforced the parents' feeling that Shelly was, indeed, a creature from a different order who defied the usual systems of classification. Even so, life with Shelly was wonderful, with the joys far outweighing the troubles. She seemed a luxurious tropical plant, enriching and beautifying everything. Still, by her early teens, the worries about something strange and shadowy grew to new proportions.

Shelly would stay awake at nights, busying herself with music and phone calls to a girlfriend who also slept odd hours. She started to lie, beginning with small fibs that soon grew very big. Sam and Ruth felt they knew almost nothing about her activities. They became so frightened about what might be going on behind their backs, that they had her telephone tapped and spent hours every day listening to the tapes. By this time, she was spending many nights away from home. The parents' attempts to stop her were met by torrents of abuse. She laughed brazenly to their faces: "Talk, talk, talk! All you can do is talk!" She was sent to a psychologist and when they asked her about the session, she said in the same dismissive tone, "Words, words, words!"

Shelly had many fears, some explicit, others vague. She was afraid of school and often refused to go, especially when there were exams. Another of her constant fears was that her parents would divorce, which was a real possibility. Sometimes, however, Shelly would panic without being able to say why. Sam and Ruth felt that the fears came from her shadowy inner world, from which they felt excluded. Hoping that a psychologist would unveil the mystery, they tried to convince her to go to therapy. They offered her pleasure trips, to Disneyland and then to the Olympic games, if she were willing to go. Shelly went to a few sessions, but stopped, right after the trip. She also agreed to a psychiatric examination (which cost the parents a stereo system). The psychiatrist's contribution was to say that Shelly was a serious suicide risk.

Shelly had a deep wish to belong and would come to school (even at the height of her fears), if only to keep in touch with her friends. Despite her goodwill, however, she was gradually developing a reputation for weirdness and becoming more and more isolated. She ended up with the one girlfriend with whom she talked at night, who was also considered "weird."

It was the conversations with this friend that the parents were tapping. But all their eavesdropping failed to make things any clearer. In one of their conversations, Shelly's friend proposed that they prostitute themselves in a high-class hotel. The parents could not decide whether the proposal had been made in earnest. In fact, despite their endless listening, they felt as much in the dark about Shelly's "real" world as before.

The parents approached our program in a mood of profound dejection. Shelly was staying out almost every night and sleeping most of the day. Lately, she all but refused to talk to them, except when she wanted to express her sarcasm. The parents told the therapist that they had tried everything, including a radical change in their stance toward Shelly. Sam, whom Ruth described as "soft as melting butter," had lost his bearings and, on one occasion, used physical force, pushing Shelly into her room and keeping her locked in for hours. He had been surprised at his own response and even more at Shelly's reaction: she behaved quite respectfully, for a few days. Ruth, on the other hand, who had always been stricter and more demanding, tried the soft tack. Ironically, the parents' efforts seemed almost calculated to cancel each other. However, neither parent believed that these changes would bring about any improvement. They were sure that, like their previous attempts, the recent ones would founder against Shelly's mysterious core.

Sam and Ruth were preparing themselves for the worst: the loss of Shelly. Sam only hoped that Shelly would not opt for self-destruction as her way out of their lives. It seemed as if the story were coming full turn: Shelly had entered their lives from another world and was slipping back into another world. This was the cue for the therapist's message about parental presence.

I feel quite strongly that, just as you suffer from the black hole that is being left in your lives by Shelly's growing absence, Shelly suffers from your absence. I believe that what Shelly wants, more than anything else in the world, is for you to be there. Only your unshakable presence can give her the security she so desperately needs. You have, of course, tried very hard to show that you care for her: you have listened to her, reasoned with her, and told her you love her. When this failed to solve the problem, you went to professionals. They, too, talked to her and tried to get her to talk. All of this was not enough, however, because, in her eyes, words are not presence. Maybe, on the contrary, they have come to signify absence. She says so herself: 'Words, words, words! Talk, talk, talk! That's all you can do!' What we need, instead, is to replace the words by acts that will prove to her that you are concretely present.

If you agree to this course, you will have to invest a lot of time. But it will be time spent doing actual things, not listening to tape recordings in the dark. By being concretely present, you can reduce Shelly's fears. There will be hardships and I want you to use all the help I can give you, so don't hesitate to call me at any time for the duration of the treatment. If you are willing to commit yourselves, and to guarantee that you will give this task the highest priority for the coming months, we can get down to the details.

Upon receiving Ruth and Sam's full agreement, the therapist continued:

> *Your first mission will be to find where she spends the time she is away from home. Then, when she fails to come home at the stipulated hour, you go and fetch her. Go for her wherever she may be. Once at home, stay with her until she starts negotiating. Don't leave her alone, and don't go back to your usual business, even if it takes days. You can take turns arranging things, but one of you must stay with her, always. What is best, however, is that both of you stay. You can get practical help from friends and relatives. Everybody should be notified of the plan.*
>
> *This will be the first step in your parental return. She will then have her first taste of your renewed presence. Pretty soon, you will see that she will start borrowing from your strength to fight her fears. Don't expect a quick solution, however. There will be plenty of trouble, but the trouble will offer you new opportunities for making yourselves present.*

Ruth asked what they should do about Shelly's verbal abuse. With the therapist's encouragement, they decided to react by confiscating her stereo for three days. They soon had occasion to apply the sanction and the abuse vanished. Sam and Ruth felt encouraged by this first success: they could take action after all!

The real drama, however, began when Shelly failed to return from a discotheque at the stipulated time. Failing to find her in the multitude, Sam and Ruth asked the manager to summon her through the loudspeaker. Shelly was thunderstruck to find her parents there. She entered the family car, with two other friends whom Sam and Ruth had agreed to take home (writing down their respective names and addresses). Once they were back at home, Shelly declared she was leaving the house and started packing. She changed her mind, however, and went to sit on the balcony's railing (the apartment was on the fifth floor). When Sam and Ruth approached, she threatened to jump. Ruth called the therapist, who told them to stay by her and say that they would not give her up. After a while, Shelly started to make threatening movements. Sam, who was at arm's distance, grabbed her, hugged her strongly for a second, and took her to her room. He laid Shelly in her bed and sat by her without a word. Thus they remained for almost four hours. Shelly then said softly, "Dad, let me be by myself, I want to sleep!"

Shelly was still sleeping when her parents met with the therapist early in the morning. He told them that the act of pulling her, hugging her, and staying with her in the room had been a powerful way of saying, "We are bringing you back! You belong with us!"

The storm, however, was just beginning. Sam and Ruth went home with a decision not to let things go back to normal until a contract had been negotiated, stipulating new rules of conduct. The therapist encouraged them to keep Shelly at home for as long as it took, inviting relatives and friends to help in the negotiation. They closed the two exits of the apartment, unscrewed the bathroom lock, and waited for Shelly to wake up. Shelly screamed, then threatened, then started to throw things about. She worked herself up to shattering her window and her mirror. Sam grabbed her and held her down until she stopped fighting. She then started screaming again. The neighbors complained, but nobody called the police. Shelly only became quiet with the arrival of her parents' friends and relatives.

She refused to speak, however, until late in the night, when she declared she wanted to leave the house. They phoned the therapist, who invited them all to a session in the morning. Shelly came in, sulking. When asked what she wanted, she said she wanted to leave the house. The therapist offered to contact a boarding school. Shelly said she was not going to a boarding school but to her grandmother's house. The parents said she could not go to her grandmother's. Shelly then threatened to kill the therapist. In any case, she said she did not care because she was going to kill herself soon. The therapist told the parents that they would have to stay with her until they were sure she was no longer suicidal. The session was concluded on this note.

By the end of the day, Shelly had declared she had decided to stay home. The parents replied that this would require a series of rules: there would be no physical or verbal abuse, she would have to inform them continuously of her whereabouts, she could go out only with permission, and would take private lessons to make up for what she had missed at school. Shelly, on her side, succeeded in gaining some leeway on the subject of her outings. The negotiations were concluded by dawn. Upon waking up, the parents were surprised to find the breakfast table set for the two of them. Shelly said she had already eaten. She sat on a sofa, looking pleased as her parents ate. She was still somewhat apart, but no longer in a different world. There were still hardships in the offing, but Shelly's parents felt that they knew better how to react.

Prize and Punishment

In spite of an impressive research record, behavioral programs centered on prize and punishment are sometimes unattractive to parents and to therapists. Some view them as a form of bribery, while others find fault with their mechanical nature. However, prize and punishment can be made into powerful carriers of parental presence when used with a new emphasis.

A "Time-in"

Consider, for instance, the behavioral technique of *time-out*. The procedure consists of a behaviorally specified target (e.g., temper tantrums) and of a time-out procedure (e.g., sending the child to the bathroom for five minutes whenever the target behavior occurs). Once these elements are defined, the program can, in principle, work quite impersonally: each instance of the target behavior needs to be followed by the time-out procedure. It does not matter who does the punishing. In contrast to this, consider the use of time as exemplified in this chapter. Rather than sending the child away, the parents stay with the child for as long as it takes to reach the desired outcome. Moreover, only the parents can carry out the procedure, since the message to be conveyed is, "We are here!" Although this procedure is also a kind of punishment, its interpersonal impact is completely different. To underline the difference from the behavioral *time-out*, we might call our procedure *time-in*.

The Pawnbroker

The use of prize and punishment as a tool of parental presence is also shown in a strategy nicknamed *the pawnbroker* (Price, 1997). The parents decide on a sum of money to be given to the child each week if the child abides by certain rules. The money is put in a jar (or a figure representing the sum is put on display) and the rules are explained to the child. With each infringement, the sum is reduced by a given amount. The child not only may lose the whole sum, but also may incur a debt, in which case the parents take away some article that belongs to the child, exchanging it for a "pawnbroker slip." The child can have the article back, but only by repaying the debt.

It might seem that this procedure turns the parents into anonymous accountants. Not necessarily, however. First of all, it is the parents who decide what constitutes an offense. When haggling begins, the parents can say, "That's the way I see it, so that's the way it will be!" The parents' judgment is thus returned to center stage. The parental activities of observing, judging, rewarding, and punishing thus become no less important than the rewards and punishments. We can thus tell the parents, "It is not the prize or the penalty alone that does the job, but rather that *you* set the rules, *you* are the arbiter, and *you* dole out the retribution." Rather than being an anonymous technique, the program actually redeems the parents from anonymity.

> *The mother of twins (aged 9) confiscated the girls' dolls when they contracted a debt the size of half of their weekly prize. After a week, the girls succeeded in redeeming the toys from the "pawnbroker's." They hugged and kissed the dolls, comforting them, and telling them they would never leave them alone again. The girls played out this "family reunion" in the mother's presence. Although the event's surface text speaks of rewards and penalties, the underlying text deals with parental absence and renewed presence.*

Chapter Four

◆

Systemic Presence

Parents are endowed with *systemic presence* to the extent that they experience themselves and are experienced by their children as being backed and confirmed by others. Indeed, parents do not act in a vacuum but are influenced by one another and by the people, institutions, and culture in which they live. Parental presence can be drained by conflict, sabotage, and indifference or fed by confirmation and support. The therapist's task is to help parents to spot and stop the systemic leaks in parental presence and to find ways of increasing the positive systemic flow.

Parental Aloneness and Lack of Support

Among victimized parents there is a high proportion of single, divorced, and widowed mothers. The mother who rears her children by herself may have good reasons for feeling weak: she may be physically unequal to her sons or daughters, be overworked to the point of exhaustion, or suffer from the chronic insecurity of the lonely. Lack of support may also characterize couples who are formally intact: marital war can be worse than aloneness.

In order for support to be helpful, it must be geared to uphold, rather than replace, the lonely parent. Any assistance, no matter how well meaning, that implies that the parent is incompetent can only deepen parental absence. This may be just as true when a caretaker is introduced into the home as when a psychotherapist is put in charge of the child's mental health. In both cases, there may be a down side to getting the help.

In our program, we begin by making ourselves available for emergency calls. For the lonely parent, the possibility of discussing burning issues can be an invaluable resource. Therapist availability, however, should be viewed as only a partial and temporary device to be abetted and replaced by help from other sources.

Lonely parents often get caught in a self-defeating syllogism:

> *I am helpless and lonely.*
> *Nobody loves the helpless and lonely.*
> *Therefore I must stay helpless and lonely.*

To break this negative spiral, a search must be made for sources of support in the familial and extrafamilial environment. The therapist may offer aid in inviting and persuading possible helpers. Most parents decline this offer, choosing to do so by themselves. Sometimes, it is the very offer of help by the therapist that triggers their decision to search on their own.

Once the request for help is clearly expressed, support often becomes available. Thus, a friend or relative who is willing to help a single mother who lives in physical fear of her child can often be found: we request that the helper stay with the mother during the critical stages of treatment (sometimes only for a couple of "hot" hours a day) and intervene in the mother's favor only if she is physically attacked. The very presence of another person has an inhibiting effect on the child's aggression. The mother may then feel doubly encouraged: she was found worthy of help and her fear of attack was relieved. A program of action that had seemed all but impracticable may then be launched. Of course there is the fear that the moment the protector leaves, things will go back to square one. By then, however, the mother may feel less helpless and appear to the child in a new light.

> *The elderly parents of a violent 16-year-old boy accepted the suggestion of a family therapist to place an ad in the newspaper requesting the services of a soldier newly released from the army, in return for free lodging. A number of candidates applied and were interviewed by the parents. They chose a brawny and kindly ex-parachutist. His job was to be in the house at the critical hours when the boy returned from school and in the evening and, if the need arose, to prevent the child from hitting the parents without, however, hitting him back.*
>
> *When the boy came home from school, he found the new lodger in the dining room, watching TV, eating peanuts, and doing a series of pushups. When the boy asked his parents about the guest, they replied evasively that it was someone they had taken in for their own private reasons. The lodger's mere presence in the house put a stop to the physical violence.* He never had to lift a finger. As a fringe benefit, he became the boy's sports' coach. He left after three months, but remained in touch with the family and with his young trainee. The violence did not return.*

A related issue is whether or not to ask the police for help: understandably, parents are reluctant to file a complaint. They fear they will incur the child's unending hatred or stigmatize the child for life. There is also the lurking fear that the child might be ill treated. The police thus appear as a veritable Pandora's box.

---

* Dr. Baruch Scholem

One possible way to address these fears is to contact, in advance, the probation officer who would be in charge of the child, in case the parents file a complaint. This extension of the therapeutic net to include the probation officer can do much to reduce the parents' feelings of anonymity and potential arbitrariness. In the following case, the police were involved without the mediation of a probation officer, with mixed results.

Case 6: To Call or Not to Call the Police

David, the 18-year-old only son of Leah and Adam (both in their late 50s), was a body builder. He was raised like a prince but, to his parents' grief, grew up to be a tyrant. Lately, he had developed a peculiar way, besides the usual threats and breakage, of manifesting his displeasure toward Leah: using his chest, he would push her up against the wall. Despite David's bullying, however, Leah remained soft and forgiving. Adam, on the other hand, became sullen and withdrawn. They approached our program when both had reached the conclusion that the situation was unbearable.

Even Leah could see that David was a better person when he was not at home. He was sociable, a good pupil, and a steady worker. Recently, he had even managed to buy himself a motorcycle with the money he had earned working in a gas station. The moment he entered the house, however, a monstrous change would occur. Adam would withdraw to his room and Leah would stay on to cook his dinner and iron his clothes. She was getting fed up, however, and was thinking seriously about getting David to move out of the house. Adam and Leah seemed to be at one in this, despite their wide-ranging disagreements in other areas.

Both thought that David would probably agree to move out with their financial help. He had raised the idea himself. However, at other times he said he would never move out. There were also fears that David might plunder the house before leaving. He had already stolen money from Leah's purse and, before buying the motorcycle, had often taken Adam's car without his permission, once parking it for three days far from home, to punish his father for some unpleasantness. Leah and Adam feared that David might use threats and violence to get more money for an apartment. Adam wondered about going to the police, if this happened. Leah had already twice summoned the police but, when they arrived, she dismissed the whole thing. The therapist said that such a step might be helpful, if thoughtfully carried out. However, acting on the spur of the moment, particularly if the complaint was canceled right away, might do more damage than good.

The therapist gave them a letter that, in case they decided to file a complaint, could be shown to the police officer. From our previous experience, we knew that some officers would try to get rid of a complaining parent by sending him or her to a psychologist. The letter would preempt this outcome, by asking the police to take the parents' complaint seriously. The therapist also wrote the parents a summary of his impressions, which was read to Adam and Leah at the next session. A copy was sent to David, with the parents' agreement, so as to show him that they were no longer alone.

> I want to summarize my impressions about the difficulties between you and David. I am sending a copy of this letter to David, too, for I think he should be informed about your decision to ask for help concerning him.
>
> David poses a riddle: is he a successful young person or a mixture of baby and bully? The evidence goes both ways. On the one hand, he has proved that he can be popular, earn money, and study well. He has also shown that if he has a real goal, he is capable of persevering. Thus, he is the only one of his group of friends who has succeeded in buying a motorcycle through his own efforts. On the other hand, there are also signs of the baby/bully. Thus, at home, he gets his way by means of

threats, tantrums, and thefts. He has also pus?
around, especially Leah. These are the acts of a bully.
that he cannot contain his temper, when provoked. That's ?
baby/bullies usually say. I have no doubt that if he always be-
haved like that, he would have been fired long ago. He would
also have lost his driver's license and, probably, his friends.

Maybe the solution to the riddle is that David is a grown-up
outside and a baby/bully at home. If so, maybe he is a baby/
bully because he can get away with it. In your behavior toward
him, Adam and Leah, you oscillate between fear and pity. The
fear paralyzes you and the pity makes you melt. The mixture of
fear and pity is very dangerous because it makes David more
and more into a baby/bully: the pity babies him and the fear
turns him ever more into a bully. Thus, he is being corrupted
by the present situation and becoming more of a baby/bully.
Sooner or later, this will spill over to the outside.

For these reasons, I think you are right that David should
leave the house. I don't know whether or not you will put your
plan into practice and whether he will agree. Whichever way
you go, however, things may get out of hand and you may need
police protection. To this end, I am also giving you a letter to
the police, so that if and when you decide to file a complaint,
the police will take it seriously and proceedings will be started
to get David out of the house. I will be glad to be of any ad-
ditional help.

Even as the therapist read Leah and Adam the message, their
solidarity began to crack. Adam grew more decided, but Leah
asked tearfully, "If David leaves the house, who will cook for
him?" Leah's readiness to act was quickly melting into motherly
pity. Adam decided to call an end to the session. He said they
would have to talk things over before deciding whether another
session was necessary. However, both agreed that the letter
should be sent to David.

weeks later. Leah answered and
...uch better. She told the therapist
...ng to the police: "I am a mother,
...y that Adam had already done pre-
...ne session, David had threatened to
... police and filed a complaint. David
...ation house and proceedings were ini-

...known to the therapist only four months
later. A... therapist and told him that he had, at the
time of the sessi... d a complaint on the grounds of threat, theft,
and physical attack. The impact on David was dramatic. He
stopped all violence, both physical and verbal. Adam said that the
change was beyond belief: David had become helpful and considerate. There was only one problem left. Following David's change,
Adam had decided to cancel the complaint. He had gone to the police, but they told him that the file had already been processed and
that David would soon be summoned to stand trial. He wrote
letters and petitions, but to no avail. He asked the therapist if he
could help. It was too late. The letters sent by the therapist were
answered in the negative. Had David been a minor, the case
would have been under the care of a juvenile probation officer
and things would probably have taken a different course.

David did not change for the worse when he found out that
his father was powerless to suspend the proceedings against him.
The family, however, is paying a heavy price for its gains.

Marital Conflict

A very common professional mistake when working with children and their parents is to let the therapeutic dialogue be de-
flected from parenting to marital issues. Some therapists argue
that since the parents are ineffective because of marital conflict,
there can be no real progress with the child before the marital

conflict is resolved. Another reason advanced for giving priority to marital issues is that the child's misbehavior is functional in keeping the parents together; marital therapy is, therefore, necessary to release the child from this role. These arguments are quite unconvincing:

1. Many parents succeed in cooperating on parenting issues despite deep disagreements in other areas.
2. Many parents find it easier to go on venting their marital grievances than to confront their children. By focusing on marital issues, the therapist may be doing no more than helping the parents to eschew the harder parenting tasks.
3. The child's deteriorating condition can hardly wait for the successful completion of marital therapy.

I would conclude that the best course for the therapist when the parents ask for help because of trouble with children, is to stick to the parenting issues, even in spite of the parents' attempts to push the marital conflict to the fore.

One area of marital relations, however, is crucial to the dialogue with parents and its consideration should never be postponed: the mutual blame, competition, and sabotage in the parents' dealings with the child. Here, a truce must be arranged and new rules negotiated. The therapist's role is to pinpoint the conflicting patterns, clarify their damage, and help the parents to find alternatives. A common difficulty in this process is that the therapist is often seen by one of the parents as the other's ally. The therapy may then become infected with the very blame, competition, and sabotage that it was supposed to overcome. To prevent this, the counselor should strive to assume a symmetrical, nonblaming position toward both parents. Parents, however, often hope for more than the mere absence of blame, wishing to be positively justified. This is a delicate situation, as each side may view the other's exoneration as tantamount to his or her own condemnation.

Once again, good use can be made of the kind of message described in the previous chapter: a dialectical succession of empathic confirmations and honest challenges. But this time each of the spouses should be equally confirmed and challenged, so that the message becomes fully symmetrical. By doing so, the therapist will gain a positive and balanced position regarding both spouses. This procedure is illustrated in the following two cases.

Case 7: A Challenge to Mutual Blaming

Lara and Boris were called to the police station because their 16-year-old daughter, Rita, had been arrested. She was caught gambling with other youngsters in a makeshift casino. To make matters worse, a large amount of marijuana was found in her possession. The parents took Rita home and discovered that she had a lot of money in her purse. They suspected her of being involved in drug traffic. They confronted her and she confessed to having stolen hundreds of dollars from them and from her grandmother.

The next day, the parents took Rita to a therapist. Rita promised to cut herself off from the companions who had gotten her involved her with drugs and gambling. Until recently, she had been quite popular at school and still had some good friends to whom she could turn. Although she seemed truly repentant and cooperative, she reacted very badly to her parents' decision to supervise her closely. She thought that her confession and her good intentions entitled her to much greater credit. Faced with this attitude, the therapist decided to see the parents and Rita apart for a few sessions.

In the first session with the parents, a longstanding pattern of mutual blame emerged: Lara accused Boris of always being too critical of Rita and Boris accused Lara of being too lax. Lara demanded that Boris become more accepting and Boris countered by demanding that Lara back him up with stricter rules. Both attributed Rita's condition to the other's mistakes. This seesaw threatened to paralyze the treatment. After one more session had been wasted on mutual accusations, the therapist sent the parents the following letter.

After our last meeting, I asked myself what the problem was with your attempts to deal with Rita. I reached the conclusion that although you both have positive parental wishes and attitudes, in your attempts to realize them, you achieve the very opposite of what you intend.

To begin with you, Lara: your reactions toward Rita spring from your motherly feelings. You feel one with Rita's pain and suffer with her suffering. When you accede to her desires, it is not out of mere weakness, but out of conviction that Rita needs love and warmth as much as demands and rules. These feelings are your own way of being a mother: betraying them would be like betraying yourself. If this is so, how is it that you seem so ineffective? How can it be that far from helping Rita to build herself, you may actually be allowing the opposite to happen? I think there are two reasons for this paradoxical outcome: one has to do with Rita and one with Boris.

Rita often experiences your warmth as pity. This is a very negative experience: being pitied, for her, is the same as being inferior. She feels that you stoop to her in your love, rather than showing her respect. She is then left with two options, both negative: she may either accept your pitying love and believe that she deserves it because she is weak and incapable; or she may reject it, exploiting it for her purposes. In the first case, her self-esteem sinks, in the second, her morals. With Boris, also, you get the opposite of what you bargained for: you would like him to become more accepting and warmer. However, the more you are driven by pity, the more Boris becomes convinced that only he can show Rita what really lies in store for her. Boris thus becomes more critical and demanding. This is the exact opposite of what you desired.

What about you, Boris? In your wishes for Rita, you show yourself as a caring father: you want her to stop cheating herself and to take an honest look at her situation. If she doesn't, you fear her fate is sealed. This is the reason for your "nudging" and for your rejection of Rita's and Lara's attempts to prettify things: you feel that you are the only one who dares speak the truth. So, why does your attempt backfire? The reason lies in the reactions that you cause in Lara and Rita. When you speak your mind to Rita, Lara feels compelled to compensate, as she believes that Rita must then feel unloved and unsupported. Thus, you actually increase her pity. As for Rita, the harsher your talk (and, at times, you do sound belittling and even scornful), the more deaf and cynical she becomes. I saw this happen more than once in the initial session: she reacted to your rising tones with a dismissive shrug. This cynical response is one of the worst dangers for a girl like Rita: it may blind her to everything positive.

What can the two of you do? Is there any way out of this crazy dance? What is clear to me is that if you, Lara, could find ways to show your love to Rita without letting it turn into pitiful softness, and if you, Boris, could speak your mind without scorn, you might be able to hold to your different ways and voices profitably. More: if you could stop blaming and disqualifying each other, you might even surprise yourselves by, occasionally, changing places: your turn, Boris, would then be to enjoy being close, and yours, Lara, to show some constructive strictness. Rita would, of course, profit greatly from this richer pattern.

The message set the stage for the coming sessions. After a few weeks, the disputes between Lara and Boris were much reduced.

Rita's stormy behavior, however, brought the parents (and the therapy) again and again to the test. Sometimes, Boris and Lara would slip back for a while into mutual accusations. The therapist, however, succeeded in weathering these storms, not in the least because of the parents' conviction that he accepted them both and was partial to neither. The symmetrical message of mutual confirmation and challenge had gained him this standing. It also allowed him considerable leeway in dealing sometimes with Lara's and sometimes with Boris' one-sidedness: they both knew that no matter who happened to be in the hot seat, the therapist's basic attitude was balanced. After about eight months of intensive work, the parents and Rita felt much more confident about the future.

Case 8: A Challenge to Hate

When Bernard was 16, he had his first epileptic seizure. He was diagnosed promptly but he continued to suffer occasional *grand mal* seizures in spite of medical treatment. He was extremely attached to his routines and reacted violently to their slightest infringement on the part of his parents (Mel and Hannah) or sisters. The family lived under continuous threat. If they failed to buy the right brands of food in the exact specified quantities; forgot to tape record the soap opera to which he was addicted; moved any objects in his room; or were too talkative when he required quiet, they knew what to expect: he would scream, hit, and throw things about. Sometimes, he would have his tantrum in the middle of the night. He once wounded his father with a piece of china.

Hannah and Mel, who had been considering divorce before Bernard became epileptic, felt trapped. They feared that Bernard's condition would worsen and that he might attempt suicide if they separated. Hannah also believed that since she and Mel were always fighting about Bernard, he would blame himself for the divorce. Actually, Bernard was not the only violent person in the house. The fights between Hannah and Mel sometimes escalated into mutual blows.

Hannah had had a radical change of attitude toward Bernard since he had become ill: although she had often been harsh and demanding in the past, she now went out of her way to cater to his every whim, also regimenting the other family members to this end. She blamed Mel for Bernard's condition, accusing him of destroying the last remnants of Bernard's self-esteem by calling him names and telling him that he wished he had never been born. Mel, in turn, called Hannah *Bernard's henchwoman* and argued that she made little of his capabilities. For instance, in spite of his medical condition, he was accepted by the army as a volunteer (this is not unusual in Israel) and had no uncontrollable outbursts when away from home. Hannah did not contest the facts, but attributed all of Bernard's outbursts to Mel's verbal violence.

All the therapist's attempts to make Mel and Hannah agree on any line of action concerning Bernard were brought to naught by their mutual hostility. The therapeutic sessions became just another arena for their brawls. Unable to get a word in edgewise, after a few sessions, the therapist sent them the following letter.

> *After our last session, I came to think that there is a compelling logic behind your behavior. Both of you find it almost impossible not to be carried away by indignation. You, Hannah, cannot but react with endless anger, or even hate, when Mel says such cruel things to your son. You, Mel, cannot but feel that the whole family is living under a reign of terror, because of Bernard's dictates and of Hannah's policy of unconditional surrender. These feelings are perfectly justified, and so are your goals. I think that, under different conditions, you might succeed in achieving both of them.*
>
> *The tragic irony is that, in spite of your positive desires, you both end up by getting the contrary of what you bargained for.*

Thus, Hannah, in your attempts to establish an atmosphere of acceptance, you only succeed in deepening the hatred within the family. I believe that, in the end, Bernard may suffer much more from the hatred in which you are all steeped, than from Mel's verbal violence. Mel's diatribes are hurled to Bernard's face. The hatred, however, works underneath the surface, like a continuous poisoning.

You, Mel, in your attempts to break free, succeed only in making the terror worse. Each of your rebellious attempts toward Bernard or Hannah is followed by a harsh punishment in which the whole family pays a heavy price. Instead of getting more freedom, you get more hatred. The greater your anger, Mel, the more that Hannah will hate you. The greater your indignation, Hannah, the more that Mel will hate you. Today, it seems that the two of you are so shackled by hatred that every attempt to come loose only tightens the bind.

I believe that most of the suffering in the family is due to hatred. But can you change this? Do you have any control over it? Are you not inexorably pulled by it against your will and reason? Is it not your tragic fate to go on hating and hating? I have no answer to this. Sometimes, it seems to me that we feed our hatred and allow it to take over. Sometimes, I feel that hatred simply snatches us with its mighty hand. In the end, each of you alone will have to find the answer to this question: whether it is your fate to surrender to hatred or to rescue yourselves, your son, and your daughters from its grip.

The message had a powerful impact: Hannah and Mel were both hurt and frightened by the imputation of hatred. They tried to say that they were only reacting and had no intention of causing gratuitous pain. Mel was the first to take a real step: he decided to avoid all clashes with Bernard and did so with almost saintly fortitude. Hannah reacted in kind: she stopped blaming Mel for having caused Bernard's condition. She also stopped pressuring the family to fulfill Bernard's demands: she did what she could on her own, without forcing the others to help her. Bernard, in turn, became less explosive as Hannah and Mel stopped fighting over him.

The improvement in the home atmosphere released Mel from the feeling of entrapment and, after a few months, he left the house and started divorce proceedings. Hannah reacted furiously, accusing him of leaving her alone to bear the brunt of Bernard's illness. However, soon she was surprised to discover that with Mel out of the way, she dared to behave more assertively toward Bernard.

A year later, Bernard was doing far better than either Hannah or Mel had ever imagined he would. He passed his high school exams and was working hard to go to college. Hannah was also enjoying the fruits of her belated divorce and, for the first time in five years, decided she could do without therapy.

Parents, School, and Peers: Interfaces

Scott W. Henggeler (1996) is the master of the interface. In his multisystemic approach to the treatment of children with behavior disorders, he shows how the imaginative creation of unlikely encounters with and between the different subsystems that involve the child—such as parents, school, and peers—may lead to quite unexpected outcomes.

A 15-year-old girl was being ostracized by her schoolmates because she smelled bad. The therapist drove over to the girl's house to try to bring the girl's mother to a meeting with the teacher. The mother was a dirty, disheveled, and haggard woman, who lived with her seven children in a house trailer with no running water. The teacher was an upper-middle-class neatly dressed woman with ultrapolished manners. On the way to the meeting, the therapist noticed that the mother was carrying a bag with something that looked suspiciously like a butcher's knife. The therapist asked about the knife and the mother replied that if words failed to do the job, the knife might come in handy. The therapist succeeded in convincing the mother to leave the knife in the car and in getting the mother and teacher to communicate. In spite of the very inauspicious beginnings, the outcome was positive for the girl, the mother, and the teacher. (Henggeler, 1996, pp. 190–191)

A 14-year-old girl who had been caught shoplifting (together with two girlfriends) was talked into bringing her friends to a meeting with the therapist in a fast-food restaurant. The therapist got the three girls interested in a new kind of adventure: looking for part-time jobs. He taught them how to fill out applications and coached them for the upcoming interviews. After a few weeks, the three were employed. The therapist then helped the girls and their parents to negotiate the use of their paychecks. (Henggeler, 1996, p. 162.)

These outcomes of these stories may seem like fairy-tale endings. Although Henggeler does not present them as typical, they do suggest some untapped therapeutic possibilities. Research confirms this hope: the multisystemic approach holds what is probably the best record in the treatment of juvenile delinquency, in terms both of reduction in criminal behaviors and of improvement in the home atmosphere. (Henggeler, Rodick, Borduin, et al., 1986) The following case shows how Henggeler's ideas can be put into practice in the service of parental presence.

The 8-year-old son of a divorced Russian woman refused, after living in Israel for only nine months, to speak to her in Russian. He was already fluent in Hebrew and a good pupil at school. The mother, who could hardly frame one sentence in Hebrew, became a laughingstock in his eyes. She held her peace, however, because of the boy's successful adaptation to the new surroundings. But when he began to steal money from her purse, she decided to ask for help. She was referred to a school psychologist who had come from Russia five years earlier.

A plan was developed in which the boy's teacher or the school principal would phone the mother each day to report on the boy's progress and behavior at school. The boy would also be given a weekly report in Russian (which he could not read), to be signed by the mother. In turn, the mother would send, through her son, weekly reports (in Russian, of course) on his home behavior to the therapist. The therapist would peruse the reports and make pertinent comments. To cap this round of confirmatory contacts, the mother was invited to accompany the boy and class on the major school outing of the year. Her standing in the boy's eyes, and in her own, improved tremendously. Growing more sure of herself, the mother, a mathematician by training, started to teach her son tricks with numbers, with which he amazed his teacher and classmates.

Presence Nets

Consider the following situations:

1. The parents of a 15-year-old girl, who had twice run away from home, contacted her friends, friends' parents, teachers, school principal, and the manager of the discotheque she frequented to ask for their help in stopping her from running away.
2. The father of a 17-year-old girl who was getting hooked on cocaine brought four of her friends (who were not drug users) to a session with the therapist. The therapist helped her father and friends to set up a monthlong watch to prevent the girl from taking drugs.

3. The pregnant wife of a 19-year-old boy told his parents that their son was planning to commit suicide. The parents invited everybody who cared for the young man to beg him not to go through with his plan. Among the supplicants (besides the wife and parents) were his sisters (ages 10 and 6), elementary school teacher, grandparents, and mother-in-law.

In all of these cases, the establishment of the net proved to be a turning point. A moving case in White and Epston (1990) may help us understand why.

Haare, a 13-year-old Maori boy, had lost, within a few months, both of his grandparents, who had brought him up; had dropped out of school; and had grown apathetic and had stopped taking his medication for asthma. His mother, who was not yet 30, worked and lived in another city and had had little contact with Haare, but returned to take care of him. Haare had been hospitalized six times with acute respiratory crises. The head of the ICU said that he had survived by luck, but that unless he took his medication, he was condemned. The mother and two cousins had tried, to no avail, to get Haare to comply.

David Epston, who had been approached by the mother, told her that since it was a matter of life and death, he could only accept responsibility for the case if she brought 20 members of the extended family to the coming session. The mother brought in the 20 people, plus Haare. Epston told the family that Haare had lost the will to live, and that their job was to prevent him from dying. After a heated debate, the family decided that Haare should stay with his mother, but that she should get all the help she needed from the family.

A program was set up for helping Haare to develop a daily routine and go back to school. Haare's cousins and uncles would be in charge of helping him out with his school tasks and

taking him to outings. Other relatives volunteered to help Haare
prepare an album to perpetuate the memory of his grandparents.
The grandparents thus joined the net in a symbolic way. A plan
was also devised for supervising Haare's intake of medication.
He recovered quickly, had no more life-threatening crises, and
was doing well at a five-year follow-up (White & Epston, 1990,
pp. 86–88).

We should note that previously there had been no dearth of
well-intentioned attempts to help Haare. However, now things
were doubly different: (a) the disparate efforts were woven into
a net and (b) the net upheld the mother. It is the confluence of
these two processes that is invaluable for supporting parental
presence.

At a given moment in its growth, an expanding social net
will achieve a critical mass that makes for a qualitative change.
It is as if the net has come to symbolize the world. Thus, if *the
net* expresses care, *the world* is no longer indifferent. Haare's
world was no longer empty. For the purpose of parental presence it is meaningful that the net was convened *by the mother*
and worked *through the mother*. Thus, a *parents' net* is required in which the members act as the parents' agents and rep-
resentatives. Such a net can be a powerful source of parental
presence.

One of the net's chief tasks is to award the seal of social ap-
proval to the parents' initiatives. Say that the parents were to
undertake, by themselves, something highly unusual, such as entering a club in the middle of the night to search for their adolescent son or daughter. In all probability, the teenager would
view such an act as a unique, crazy gesture. If, however, the same
act were performed before a chorus of supportive and confirming
voices (of, for example, relatives, friends, and teachers), it would
no longer be an isolated, weird event but a new reality to be

reckoned with. The net has thus endowed the act with substance: the parental gesture has grown to the status of a new rule.

In fact, it is not always necessary to have a very large net to achieve impact. For many, a local change or a small supporting cast may do. The small net's confirmatory impact can then be enhanced, say, by writing and circulating a report or by repeating the story to others. However, at those critical junctures where a tragic outcome is at stake (when a child attempts suicide, is caught in criminal activities, or runs away from home), the gathering of a large net with a critical mass capable of defining a new reality becomes justified. It may then be a waste of therapeutic opportunity to make do with less.

> A 16-year-old boy succeeded in coercing his parents into buying him a motorcycle by a mixture of promises and blackmail that culminated in a suicide threat. Soon after getting the motorcycle, he was badly hurt in an accident, but in two months' time, he was campaigning for a new motorcycle. This time, the parents demurred and the boy retaliated by running away from home. Two weeks later, he was seen with a known drug dealer and other marginal youths. He showed a wad of money to one of his former friends, whom he met by chance, bragging that he would soon have more than enough for a new motorcycle.
>
> The parents consulted a therapist, who asked them to bring as many relatives and friends as possible to the upcoming session. Twelve people attended. The participants were instructed on the principles of systemic presence and, in the following days, they got in touch with everybody who might know of the boy's whereabouts. Daily visits were made by net members to all the discotheques, video arcades, pool halls, and street corners in the area. Messages were left everywhere. People started to talk about the "army of baby-sitters."
>
> A week after the search was launched, the boy returned home.

He stopped keeping dubious company and renewed his links with former pals. He decided to go back to school. A month later, when he threatened to run away again, the net members were notified and the house buzzed with their presence for days. There were no more threats or signs of criminal activities.

◆

Chapter Five

Personal Presence

The establishment of parental presence involves more than the mere outward display of assertive behavior: the parents must also develop a sense that what they are doing manifests their feelings and values. *Personal presence* refers to this experience—the parents are speaking with their own voices.

Victimized parents often feel so afraid of speaking their mind that it seems as if, for them, affirming their values is proof of intrusiveness and expressing their needs is proof of egotism. Often, however, the very same parents who are weak at home are highly determined people in other circumstances. How can we understand this gap? What forces are active in dealings with one's children that may deprive even the most vibrant individual of personal presence?

One of the most common factors that stifle the parental voice is the belief that the child's behavior is due to psychopathological sources. Parents, so convinced, are prone to extremes of pity, anxiety, and guilt. These feelings, in turn, induce a sense of incompetence and a mix of appeasement and compensation that increases the problem behaviors rather than reduces them. The therapist's challenge is then to help the parents free themselves from the paralysis induced by their beliefs.

Psychopathological Beliefs

It is commonly held that demands and rules are irrelevant or noxious if the child's problem behaviors are due to deeper causes, such as traumatic experiences or unconscious conflicts. In such cases, it is assumed that therapy rather than discipline is needed. Parents are thus justified in attempting to discipline the child only when these deeper problems have been ruled out or adequately treated.

This attitude is doubly wrong. First, children who suffer from psychopathology are no less in need of rules and values than are "normal" children. The opposite actually may be true, for the more chaotic the child's inner world, the greater is the need for an orderly, stabilizing framework. Hazy or nonexistent boundaries can only aggravate the confusion. Second, moral considerations never cease being crucial in the raising of children. A child who is mentally ill must be taught, no less than a healthy one, to distinguish between good and evil. Thus, a morally unchecked schizophrenic is, in all respects, in worse condition than one who has been reared to respect the rights of others. The idea that moral development should be given a back seat to mental health is, therefore, preposterous.

Practitioners are often unaware of the possible debilitating impact of their messages. Thus, many parents who are convinced that their child's behavior is caused by unconscious conflict, repressed trauma, or developmental deficits may conclude that the correction or amelioration of the condition is a matter for the specialist. Although most therapists will deny any such implication, the parents' conclusion is understandable: if the child's behavior is due to causes that are beyond their comprehension and that can be fathomed only after years of study and clinical practice, how can they presume to deal with it? One common complaint of therapists is that the parents want them (the therapists) to fix the child in their stead. What is far less common is the awareness that, at least in part, this parental attitude has been unwittingly fostered by therapists.

In our experience, parents react very well to a redescription of the child's unruly behavior as indicative of normal human egotism and of a universal thirst for ease, pleasure, and might, rather than of trauma or pathology. Thus, the child is neither mad nor especially bad to begin with, but merely energetic, boisterous, and naturally selfish. The persistence of parental helplessness, however, may aggravate these tendencies. The parental challenge then becomes to stem what might prove to be a tide of corruption. This perspective legitimizes parental steps that would have seemed scandalous in a psychopathological frame. But are we stigmatizing the child in a new way, exchanging the psychopathological label for a moral one? We believe we are not. We are speaking about a universal tendency, which the child was smart and strong enough to realize, not about a character blemish. In effect, the parents will be better able to fight the negative trend, the more we can help them to appreciate the child's strength and cunning in the battle of survival.

The divorced mother of a 15-year-old boy described how he would empty the contents of his plate on the floor whenever her cooking failed to meet his standards. The following excerpt is taken from the second therapy session:

Mother: I can't understand why he does it! It seems perverse to me. Maybe he is afflicted with sadistic impulses. If I could only figure out what is eating him! It must be linked to what happened at the time of the divorce. He was traumatized by some very ugly scenes. Maybe he is unconsciously repeating what he saw.

Therapist: Maybe he does it because he can get away with it.

Mother: But why should he want to get away with it? It's sick!

Therapist: Many kids enjoy the exercise of their own might.

Mother: (laughing ironically) You make it sound almost desirable!

Therapist: I don't think it's sick. At least not yet. I think it thrills him to have his way. You told me he once yelled at you and threw you out of his room in front of his friends. I think that gave him a power orgasm: "See what I can do!"

Mother: Could this turn into a sexual perversion? Could he become a sadist?

Therapist: He could enjoy his total power more and more. People become addicted to these pleasures. Having one's way, always, is a deeply corruptive influence.

Mother: It's ugly! It's dangerous! He must be stopped!

The mother searched for an occasion to enter the boy's room when he was with his friends. When he screamed at her to get out of the room, she firmly asked the friends to leave, as her son was not in a condition that allowed for having guests. The friends, obviously embarrassed, left. The boy raved, but the incident proved to be a first step in the mother's recovery of her almost obliterated voice.

Pity, Guilt, and Anxiety

Parental guilt feeds parental pity and both guarantee a steady supply of parental anxiety. The three can reduce the strongest personal voice to a faint whisper.

In "To Call or Not to Call the Police" (Chapter 4), we described a mother who said she would not be a real mother if she felt no pity for her son. But would she? We believe that compassion is an appropriate feeling toward an adult son, but not pity. Compassion draws from a sense of equality ("com"=with; "passio"=suffer), whereas pity is felt for someone weaker or inferior. In compassion, the other's hurt is valued because I value my own similar hurt. Not so in pity: the other's hurt fills the whole picture and the other is not viewed as similar to ourselves. Pity thus abrogates mutuality. Parents can understand the blow to a child's self-esteem that results from pity-driven expressions and acts, for we cannot pity without conveying our view of the other as less capable. The child can then either accept our slighting messages or fight back in anger. Pity thus engenders hate of the self or of the other. For a similar reason, pity is also very different from mature love. To love our growing child as a person (and not merely as the object of our sentimentality), we must outgrow the pity that we felt when our child was still small and incapable.

As for guilt, helpless parents are often less influenced by its actual bite than by their never-ending attempts to prevent it: it is as if these parents are so averse to the very possibility of guilt that they go to any length to guarantee their innocence. Many children are masters at taking advantage of this soft parental spot.

They know that the slightest imputation of unfairness often suffices to trigger strenuous parental efforts to prove the contrary. However, parents should know that a child who feels discriminated against is never persuaded by their compensation attempts. If anything, the opposite is true: the parents' efforts only prove to the child that they must really feel in debt. Parents and child may be caught for life in this vicious circle.

> *A 75-year-old widower visited a therapist because of the insatiable demands of his younger son (age 44), who lived with him. The son had always felt discriminated against, relative to his elder sister (who was married and lived in a house of her own). Through endless complaints about the father's unfairness, he had succeeded in inducing his father to give him four cars, a generous monthly allowance (he worked intermittently), and preferential treatment in his father's will. Lately, he had started to pressure the father into putting the house in his name. The father said he had already willed the house to him. However, the son argued that his sister was sure to contest the will and, since she had money, she would end up having her way; he would remain homeless and she would be all the richer. The father gave in. The son was still not satisfied. He demanded that the father refurnish the house. During the course of a row, he said to his father: "If you cannot really love me, you might as well go live with your daughter and leave me in peace in my house!" The father called the therapist a few days later to cancel his second appointment: he had moved to his daughter's home. Hopefully, he is faring better than King Lear.*

To stop the spiraling trend of blame and appeasement, we find it helpful to start the parents on a course of *blame inoculation*. We help them realize that, whatever they do, blaming is inevitable: they will be blamed for resisting and blamed for giving in (spoiled adolescents sometimes accuse their parents of leaving them unprepared for life). Parents smile at this obvious truth and become readier to accept our other suggestions in the blaming-inoculation course:

1. They plead guilty to the child's charges, but without changing their decisions.
2. They refuse to go on discussing the matter.
3. They search for occasions for acts of *constructive unfairness* on their part.

The mother of an aggressive teenager, who had long felt unable to cope with her daughter's complaints of unfair treatment, called the therapist to say that she had just disconnected the phone in the middle of a conversation with the girl. The daughter had called her, at work, to complain about her sister's preferment and to demand compensation in that week's allowance. The mother called the therapist right after banging down the phone. Breathless with excitement, she said that she had called the therapist not only to get some encouragement, but also to keep the phone busy so as to prevent her daughter from calling back. A month later, the mother said that she was proud of her "achievements in the way of unfairness." For the first time in years, she also felt free of her chronic resentment against the daughter.

Case 9: "Unfair, but there!": Using Constructive Unfairness

Susan and Mark had five children with multiple problems, including substance abuse, obsessive-compulsive rituals, truancy, and violent tantrums. Mark complained that he had no place in the home: whatever he tried to do, Susan was sure to undermine. She always sided with the children, even against their previous joint decisions. Thus, after he and Susan had bought a skateboard for their younger son's (age 9) birthday, ruling out as unsafe a game of darts the boy had asked for, Mark found out that Susan had also bought him the darts. Sometime before, Susan had paid for an expensive trip for their second son (age 18) without consulting Mark. More recently, Susan had allowed their only daughter (age 16) to go to a jazz festival with her friends (whom the parents knew to be involved with drugs), although Mark had expressly forbidden it. On some of these occasions, Mark had reacted with physical violence against Susan.

Mark said his greatest wish was to have a real family to whom he felt he fully belonged. Susan's recurrent betrayals, however, made him feel like an outsider. Susan, in turn, said that what she wanted most was to have Mark by her side, helping out with the children. But Mark only commanded and criticized, trying to manage things by remote control. He knew that she could not stand up to the children alone. She so much as confessed that she could withstand Mark's beatings better than she could the children's pressure.

Susan's parents were Holocaust survivors. She was an only daughter and her role had been to compensate her parents for all they had suffered. Even today, when her father came to visit, Susan felt obliged to fulfill his every whim. The same happened with her children: it was as if they had taken private lessons with her parents! Susan was not happy with her role. However, she felt that Mark only made her more vulnerable to the children's demands. In the sessions, whenever Mark complained about her "betrayals," Susan would fade out. In contrast, once, when he gave her a hug, Susan stayed alert and involved.

Mark had also grown up as an only child in a bleak household of two. His father died when he was 5 and his mother remained in a state of apathetic detachment for years. He only knew about active family life from the movies and from his glimpses into other families. Children with real homes filled him with envy. He married with the intention of creating such a home, but Susan's siding with the children at his expense seemed to prove that he was doomed to a life of exclusion.

Mark and Susan felt hopelessly deprived of personal presence in the home. Mark felt banished from his rightful harbor and Susan felt robbed of her will. Both felt voiceless and alone. The therapist expressed her belief that Susan and Mark's needs were not only compatible, but mutually reinforcing: to the extent that Mark would get an effective place in the family and Susan would recover her ability to express her will; conversely, to the extent that Susan would feel herself supported, Mark would feel that he belonged. The therapist proposed a plan, involving constructive unfairness, to help Susan and Mark achieve this goal: whenever Mark felt that Susan had gone back on a joint decision, he would take the initiative to cancel her concession to the children and stay close by, to make sure that what was canceled would stay so. In each case, he would say to the affected child that what he was doing was unfair, but that he had decided to act in an unfair, fatherly manner. To show Susan (and the children) that he was not acting against her, he would take Susan on an outing each time he displayed constructive unfairness. Susan, for her part, would agree beforehand to Mark's right to make his presence felt in such a manner.

Mark warmed to the idea quickly. *Constructive unfairness* became his byword. It was soon to prove effective in strengthening a resolve that Mark had taken in a crisis with the 18-year-old son. The boy had come home, looking strange. When pressured, he confessed he had taken acid. Mark then told him, despite Susan's distress signals, that he would not be allowed to stay in the house if he took drugs. His room would be examined regularly and he would have to keep Mark and Susan informed of his whereabouts. The boy left the house in anger, staying away for two weeks.

A few days after a therapeutic session, he came home and Mark immediately entered his room and made a thorough search. To the son's complaints that he was violating his privacy, Mark replied he had decided to act in an unfair, fatherly manner. He made it clear again that if the youth wanted to stay, he would have to abide by the rules. Later that evening, he took Susan to the movies.

This event served as a model for other successful incidents. Mark, however, still criticized Susan for not taking his part more decidedly. It took him some months to recognize that she might have kept her coalition with the children at his expense had she so wanted. Susan had actually kept the door open for his incursions and had never canceled his cancellations. She beamed when he acknowledged her contribution.

Mark and Susan's relationship did not become the harmonious one they had hoped for, but there were almost no "betrayals" and there was no more violence. Mark, for his part, felt he had gained a real place in the family.

The Parental Voice

We all know the difference between an act we perform from inner conviction and one we perform out of convenience or because of external imposition. When the act is not an expression of our personal voice, we feel strained, awkward, and not fully there. When it is, we feel right and present. Of course, the same is true for parents. Unless their parenting behavior reflects their needs, feelings, and values, they are not fully there.

We, as therapists, often disregard this obvious point. For example, behavior therapists often overrule the parents' objections that reinforcement is a form of bribery; humanist therapists dismiss the parents' view that achievements are no less important than feelings; and family therapists oppose parental wishes for a deep personal involvement with the child. Our professional conscience cannot be simply put to rest with the argument that the parents' ideals are pathological. All we can say is that we, therapists, hold our therapeutic values for good and true. However, each time we force our values to prevail over those of the parents, we pay a price: the parents' acts will ring hollow to themselves and to their children.

The parents' voice will also come out stilted when they are required to behave in ways that clash with their personal styles, even if this behavior is congruent with their ideals. Thus, it is unhelpful to expect a temperamentally withdrawn father to become effusive and warm or for a happy-go-lucky mother to monitor target behaviors rigorously. Even when the parents succeed in sticking to the prescription for a while, they and the child expect the new regimen to be given up at the earliest opportunity. Children say, "They will soon tire!" and the parents say, "Until when must we go on?" For both, the program can be only a temporary device.

But does this mean that we are dooming the parents to stay as they are? Consider a family where the parents are staunch upholders of a democratic home environment; they have a natural style of spontaneous disorderliness and their major life project at the moment is to break free of their stiff upbringing. How can we help them restore their parental authority while staying true to themselves?

Fortunately, the values and styles of each and every person are multifaceted. At any time, in the inner congress of our minds, there are many strands left unused or in the shade. The therapist's job is to find, among the parents' own penchants, those that can be best harnessed to the task. Instead of proposing a "right" way of raising children, we should be searching for a fitting way for *these particular* parents to do *their* parenting more effectively. As we shall see, achieving congruence between the therapeutic program and a parent's untapped proclivities can make the difference between an anemic, unmotivated, and detached parent and an involved and decided one.

In the following two cases, the question not only was what

practical course to suggest to the parents, but, first and foremost, how to help them reassume the parenting task as an embodiment of their moral values and as an answer to their highly individual life challenges.

Case 10: Taming the Wild Dozen with Self-Prescribed Reparations

There were 12 children in this Jewish orthodox family. The eldest daughter was only 16. The father, Hershel, spent most of his day at a yeshivah [a school] studying rabbinic law. The mother, Esther, felt completely wiped out.

Esther sought the advice of the school's counseling psychologist regarding 8-year-old Joshua, who was having trouble at school. Once in the therapist's presence, however, she seemed to forget all about Joshua's problems and simply talked on and on about the impossible task of managing 12 unruly children. Getting the children to school on time or putting them to sleep was a super-human task. All fought and scrambled. Even the babies seemed eager to start walking so as to join in the rumpus. Esther would often lose her head and start hitting some of the children. Sometimes, she just collapsed on her bed. Hershel exerted more authority, but only as long as he was directly involved with the children. However, soon after arriving home, he would plunge into his books and Esther would be left alone to stem the tide.

Things had been going well until the birth of the fourth child, Isaac, who was now 13. He was the brightest of the children and a promising scholar. His teacher raved about his phenomenal memory. However, at home he was the chief troublemaker. Esther felt she was no match for him intellectually: "I am nothing compared with him!" Isaac set the example of total disobedience, which the others gleefully followed. Flouting his mother became a sport; lying became routine. Gradually, the unruliness spread to the streets. Thus, in spite of the parents' express prohibition, the elder children became very active in the national elections, heckling speakers from the opposition. When caught in the act, they lied brazenly.

Sometimes, Hershel and Esther would launch a campaign to improve the atmosphere. For example, at *Tu-Bi-Shvat*, the holiday of plants and trees, they started a "green renewal program": the plan was that the children would be told what to do only once. Prizes and punishments would be systematically meted out. The children smirked, predicting that the strategy would fail of its own accord. Esther soon found out that the bookkeeping was beyond her. The new campaign thus went the way of all previous ones.

Esther told the therapist that Hershel, as a very religious man, was wary of secular psychologists. Moreover, although he was concerned about Joshua's learning troubles, he did not think there was a problem with the other children: children were like that and the situation would sort itself out in the end. However, he agreed to meet with the therapist—but only once. Knowing that Hershel would be wary about suggestions from a secular psychologist, the therapist consulted a rabbi first.

The session began inauspiciously. Hershel gave the impression of having come to the session under duress. He answered the therapist's questions curtly, saying he did not think there was any problem with the children. Esther said that some were surely bound for trouble. Their eldest daughter, for example, was growing more and more brazen. Hershel said she was exaggerating. Esther replied that the children were already getting mixed up in street politics, in spite of their prohibition. Hershel hesitated. This was the opening the therapist was waiting for.

> **Therapist:** I would like to offer you a suggestion that might work and in which you, Esther, would not have to play the role of bookkeeper, which is bound to fail with 12 children.

Esther: Yes, I've tried recording their behavior and the children soon saw that I wouldn't hold out.

Hershel: May I say something? I guess you will tell us to set one of the children in a position of authority. We've tried that and it didn't work.

Therapist: I think I am going to propose something that you didn't try before. It may demand a lot of effort for the first month. The first stage is the real battle, the laying down of the rules, the fight for your and your wife's honor and authority. The question is whether or not you think it is worthwhile to spend a lot of time and effort to regain your children's respect.

Hershel: The question is whether or not it would work.

Therapist: I propose that every evening, say, at eight o'clock, you seat all the children, except for the babies, around the dinner table and tell them, "What we are going to do is to have each of you examine what you did today, examine your consciences, and see if you did anything wrong or bad." You say this, and you wait. If nobody speaks, you just wait. You wait and wait, keeping the children sitting. Once every hour, you ask the question again. After three hours, at 11 o'clock, you send them to bed without another word. The next evening, you start it all over again, with the same question.

Hershel: They will make fun of the whole thing. They can go on like that for the entire night.

Therapist: O.K. So, they start making fun and it goes on and on, not for the entire night, but for three hours. You control the time factor and you remain silent and serious, in spite of the giggling. The next day, you begin it all over again, so the giggling didn't achieve much.

Hershel: We have a very restless child who will start jumping around.

Therapist: You can hold him and keep him beside you.

Hershel: What will come of all that?

Therapist: Somebody will end by taking the initiative and confessing to some misbehavior. Maybe not on the first or second evening. But someone will try to see what happens if he or she confesses to a misdeed. When this happens, you ask, "How do you think you can compensate for what you did? How can you make reparations for it?" You explain to the smaller ones what "reparations" means. You just ask and wait. The waiting, the silence, and the boredom will work for you. Someone will end the waiting by confessing and proposing some reparation. You can respond that the reparation is perhaps a good idea and, after examining it for a few minutes, you tell the child that he or she is free to go to sleep. The others must stay on.

The next evening, you ask the child who confessed if the child did what he or she had agreed to do. If the child didn't do it, then he or she must find a way to guarantee that it will be done the next day. Again, you let time, silence, and boredom do the work. If they make fun, you just continue to wait. I think they will start to push each other to confess and give each other ideas for reparation. You may not believe it, but you will see it happen.

When three or four children have talked, you end the session. You don't prescribe or punish. You just ask and wait. The initiative and the control are yours, but you don't give commands or suggestions. It is the children's turn to examine their hearts and propose improvements. Gradually, a new dynamic will be started.

Hershel (in a different tone): I think you may be right. As it is now, the children stick to their childishness. But I think that the younger ones will not be able to take it.

Therapist: Maybe you should include only the children who are 5 and older. When there is an improvement in the children's behavior, you may go down to two sessions a week. Then to once a week. But it is best to go back to daily sessions if there is any backsliding.

Hershel: Why in the evening? Maybe it is better during their play time, just before it gets dark.

Therapist: The question is whether everybody is at home.

Hershel: We can make them be there. And I can then study for a few hours more in the evening.

Therapist: Good!

Hershel (after a prolonged silence): What if they are wilder the next morning because they got nervous and tired?

Therapist: Then, they will have to offer reparations for their wildness.

Hershel (again, after a long wait): What if Isaac, or his older brother, finds a way to sabotage the whole thing? Or if they vanish?

Therapist: That could be a problem, but maybe we can find a solution.

Hershel seemed doubtful. His face reflected displeasure and he kept pointing out problems. The therapist asked Hershel whether he was against the whole idea. Hershel evasively replied that he just wanted to check out the details. At the end of the session, the therapist suggested that they write down his home number so they could call at any time if they had questions. Esther wrote the number down. Hershel left the room with a polite, cold bow.

The therapist called after a week. Esther told him that "the trick" was working. It worried the therapist that she did not request another session. However, things sounded different during a follow-up call three months later. Esther recognized the therapist's voice on the phone and talked effusively for minutes:

I am so happy that you called! Blessed be God! Blessed be God! Blessed be God! You can't imagine how grateful I am. Hershel took the whole idea to heart. The children reacted well—right on the first day. We kept it up daily for three weeks! Now we

are doing it once a week. Hershel liked it so much, that now he
also comes from the yeshiva at lunchtime for a short lesson with
the children. Isaac is in charge of choosing the text and he helps
Hershel with the teaching. I would never have believed it! The
house is changed, there is not much noise, and even Joshua is
doing better at school. Blessed be God!

Hershel's critical questions and brooding silences had not been signs of resistance, after all. When I related the case to my eldest daughter, who is well versed in rabbinic writings, she told me the story of Rabbi Yohanan ben Zakkai and his pupil, Rish-Lakish: to every point in law that the master taught, Rish-Lakish would raise 24 objections; each of these objections, Rabbi ben Zakkai would meet with 24 explanations. When Rish-Lakish died, Rabbi ben Zakkai lost the love of teaching, for no pupil challenged him like Rish-Lakish. Little did we know what token of respect Hershel was conferring on the proposal! Far from reflecting resistance, his thoughtful objections were the beginning of a process of assimilation by which Hershel gradually transmuted the procedure into something truly his own. The idea of reparations had indeed tapped the very personal values that allowed Hershel to feel that he was now speaking with his own personal voice.

Case 11: Parenting a "Miracle" Child as a Child, Not as a Divine Being

Mary was an only child, born when Eva was 48 and her husband, John, was 56. John had a son, William, from a previous marriage, whom he had not seen since the child was a baby. John explained that when he discovered that his previous wife was a lesbian, he decided to cut off all ties with her and their child, fearing that if he kept in touch, he would be drawn back into the marriage. He left them with the house and his life savings. Subsequently, he married Eva, hoping that he would be able to have a family. Eva, however, did not become pregnant, until 10 years later, long after they had given up. For John, Mary was a gift from heaven—an angel, a being of joy and beauty. She was there to be adored. Eva, although not fully convinced, chimed in.

John and Eva came for help when Mary, now 4 years old, decided not to go back to kindergarten. She would stay home forever. To Mary, John was the best of friends and Eva the best of teachers. Her nanny, furthermore, was much better company than the kindergarten teachers. Mary also decreed that John and Eva could not leave the house, except for work. Why would they need other friends? She should be everything to them, and they to her. She seemed perfectly happy with things as they were. She was a joyful, pampered child.

If John and Eva wanted to go out, they had to pretend they were going to work. Mary would agree only after prolonged questioning. Sleep was another problem: Mary went to bed after midnight and John or Eva had to stay with her until she fell asleep. In addition, Mary was still bottle-fed, rejecting all solid food, except for sweets.

Eva was exhausted. She was allowed no rest, and only by endless coaxing could she win Mary's grudging agreement to turn off the lights at 11:30 P.M. Eva had to bring Mary a present every day. Mary never said "Hello!" to her, only "What did you bring today?"

In spite of all this, John and Eva were enchanted. Mary was their life. They knew she had to grow up. But how? John played with her, laughed with her, or stood in awe before her. By no means would he make her cry. The very thought was preposterous. He asked the therapist whether their coming to therapy would get Mary back to kindergarten. If so, he would come. However, if the treatment required that John cause Mary to cry, he would not collaborate.

Lately, John had grown curious and made inquiries about his son. William apparently had became a good student and athlete.

John fantasized about meeting with him and about the love that would grow between William and Mary. The therapist wondered whether John's unwillingness to frustrate Mary might not be linked to his sense of guilt for having abandoned his son. Having been bad in the past, he now had to be wholly good. On her part, Eva seemed to be well on the way to a more balanced and realistic attitude toward Mary. The following therapeutic message got the parents started.

> *Mary's birth was a miracle to you. After so many years of disappointment, she arrived like a wonder child in a fairy tale. And like fairy-tale parents, you feel you are indebted to fate and must respond in kind. Mary should stay always joyful. To frustrate her or make demands on her would be not only cruel, but ungrateful and even sacrilegious. To tell the truth, you seem to succeed quite well in your task: Mary looks happy, indeed. You describe her as laughing all the time. So how could you spoil it all by making her cry?*
>
> *And yet, this feeling is almost preventing you from being parents, for you are functioning not so much as a father and mother, but as servants. Mary may actually be growing up in a state of parental deprivation.*
>
> *Your story is very sad, for after so many years of frustrated dreams, you may be wasting the opportunity that finally came to you. You, John, suffered a similar tragedy in the past: you lost the chance to be a father. You felt you had no alternative and, to quiet your conscience, you sacrificed your life savings to your ex-wife and son. But you missed that opportunity to become a father. Your pain can still be surmised in the way you talk about your son. I believe you now have a chance of compensating for that tragedy. You have a second chance to be a father. If you miss this opportunity, your life will have been twice a tragedy.*
>
> *You, Eva, are beginning to understand that in giving in to*

Mary's every whim, you are being discounted as a person and as a mother. You have become a purveyor. To help Mary, you will have to help yourself, becoming, once again, a person with needs and boundaries. It is only by being Eva first that you can be Mary's mother.

I want you to think about this and come to a decision about the therapy. I will not be able to get Mary back to kindergarten, or to help you recover your parental and personal voices, if you set conditions or refuse point-blank to make Mary cry. She will have to cry like other children. Otherwise, she will remain an angel and will not belong to this world. She may not forgive you if this happens. If you are willing to accept this, we will be able to develop a program that will not deprive Mary of what she needs.

The message changed the atmosphere of the sessions. It had succeeded in tapping the personal experience that turned effective parenting into something the parents felt as individually meaningful to them. John began taking Mary to kindergarten daily. Eva stopped the bottle-feeding, the daily presents, and the bedtime routines. Mary responded well: she found out that children and kindergarten could be more fun than John and Eva. For a while, John thought about how he could get in touch with William. However, the fear proved stronger than the wish and he gave up on the idea.

Chapter Six

◆

Flexible Authority

Like any good principle, the idea of parental presence sometimes may be applied too rigidly. This often happens as the power struggle escalates, with parent and child becoming more and more entrenched in their respective positions. The interaction is then in danger of deteriorating into a naked fight over power. This is precisely what must be prevented. Although power issues cannot be avoided, the parents' goal should be the achievement of presence and not the child's unconditional surrender. Parental presence is essentially a dialogic concept: the parent aspires to become present in an ongoing interaction with the child. It thus would be nonsensical to further parental presence by abolishing filial presence! When a negative spiral is established, it is necessary to change course. In effect, the recovery of parental authority is seldom a straightforward process: how could it be, when the would-be opponent also happens to be the main object of the parents' care?

The typical symptoms of a negative spin are easy to recognize:

1. Parent and child respond to each other ever more punitively.

2. All positive interactions disappear.
3. Parent and child evolve a stereotyped, negative view of each other.

When assessing these phenomena, we must consider not only their emergence, but also their persistence. Some negative reactions are to be expected, once a previously helpless parent begins to take matters in hand. What should be prevented is not their appearance, but their becoming chronic fixtures.

The ability to acknowledge a mistake and to shift gears is not a sign of weakness or of lack of determination. On the contrary, it is the person who lacks confidence who often feels threatened by any change in course. At the beginning of the counseling process; parents often feel too insecure to be flexible. However, things change, as they become tempered by the struggle. In our experience, when parents and their child get trapped in a principled impasse in which both sides have much to lose, the readiness of parents to relinquish an unacceptable position may open up possibilities for dialogue that had been unavailable before.

How can we know whether any of the parents' positions have become so rigid that it would be better to help the parents relinquish them? The answer often has to do with feelings of humiliation. As the parents reassert their presence, the child inevitably loses power. For the child, this may also mean a blow to self-respect. If this feeling becomes dominant, an impasse arises. Something must then be done to remedy the offense.

In the seesaw of power struggles, there is a tendency for the humiliated to humiliate when their turn comes. Parents are not inured to this temptation. Thus, in fighting for their standing, parents often come to express their new demands in offensive ways that are experienced by the child as a threat to his or her individuality and self-esteem. As the child feels cornered, he or she hits back. At these junctures, acknowledgment by the parents of the child's right to a dignified solution may redress the balance and provide new options.

Sometimes, however, the impasse remains intractable, so long as the parents refrain from making a change in their actual demands. This is especially true with adolescents, for whom the issue of parental impingement is crucial. In effect, safeguarding one's privacy and choosing for one's self are among the main developmental tasks of adolescence. Parents have the parallel task of learning to make room for the child's autonomy. But for parents of rebellious children, withdrawing any of their demands may seem tantamount to abetting the process of deterioration. Isn't this the opposite of what we have been trying to achieve throughout this book?

Let us make it clear that we are speaking about cases of unyielding and dangerous impasse. The child (an adolescent or young adult) adamantly refuses to accept the parents' guidance and all parental attempts in this direction seem only to push the mutual punitiveness to more alarming levels. In such situations, the time may have come for the parents to take stock. Obviously, they must not go back to their former roles of being dupes and victims: the youngster must come to terms with the parents' right to self-protection. On the other hand, the parents must come to terms with the limits of their influence. There may be a bitter taste of failure to this bargain but also some valuable gains.

Case 12: Fighting for Boundaries Without Humiliation

After stealing money from his mother's purse, Daniel, a teenager from a religious Jewish family, jumped out of the window, took a taxi to a club, and spent Saturday evening [the Jewish Sabbath] dancing. He was finally caught by his father, Jacob, while trying to climb back through the window into his room in the early morning hours; his clothes smelled of cigarette smoke. It seems there was hardly a sin that he had not committed in the course of a few hours. [For religious Jews, traveling, smoking, and spending money are forbidden on the Sabbath. Stealing, of course, is a sin every day, and for anyone.]

Lately, Daniel had clashed with his father about religious school, which he wanted to leave. He was failing in his studies, often stayed home under false pretenses, and was completely alien to the school's sober atmosphere. Jacob, well known in religious circles, would not consider Daniel's wishes: if he failed in that school, he would be sent to another religious school. His mother, Sarah, was soft in her attitude toward Daniel, but he was very rough in return, often shutting her up with offensive epithets. Daniel also extorted money from her for fancy sneakers and jeans. After the incident at the club, Daniel declared he was no longer religious.

Daniel was not the first to rebel in the family. His elder brother, age 22, had rejected religion two years earlier and lived at home without any contact with the other family members, including Daniel. He was considered a heretic and an outcast. Initially, Jacob had raged and fumed. However, when things came to blows, Jacob chose the path of ostracism.

Now, without compromise and dialogue, the family was in danger of disintegrating. Daniel and Jacob were in no mind for either: Jacob demanded total obedience and Daniel wanted total freedom. One might well voice the need for flexibility: nobody listened. It seemed that soon there would be one more outcast in another room of the fragmented home.

A double-stage therapeutic strategy was decided upon: in the first stage (the only one, as far as Jacob was concerned), the therapist would help the father to put up a very tough parental fight. This was, in any case, the only strategy he would accept (the mother was completely weak, both in the therapy and at home). The therapist was hopeful that the very hardships of this stage might bring a change. The difficulties of the struggle might make both sides more amenable to dialogue. This would be the program's second stage.

The therapist phoned Jacob at work and asked whether he was determined to fight for his principles. He answered enthusiastically in the affirmative, whereupon he was asked to give absolute priority to the project for one month. He would have to spend many hours a day on duty and would need the help of a relative for some of the harder tasks. The father said that his brother-in-law, who lived in the same building, would agree to lend a hand. The therapist told him gravely that "one hand" might not be enough, and a meeting was called with the parents and the brother-in-law. The school principal, who had often collaborated with the therapist in the past, was made a party to the plan. The therapist, the school principal, and another therapist (as a supervisor) would be on call around the clock. The first stage was thus launched with the backing of a network of alliances.

For the coming month, Daniel would be driven to school by his father, who would also phone the school three times every morning and step in at least once more, at various hours, to make his presence felt. On the way to school (it was a 20-minute ride), the father would avoid mention of all controversial issues. Jacob would also come home from work earlier, so as to be available on the home front. A policy of strict control over money was instituted to prevent filching. New locks were installed on Daniel's window and on the front door, and the new keys were carefully hidden. Sarah's passive acquiescence was secured by making Daniel's offensive behavior toward her into one of the program's chief issues. Whenever Daniel screamed at her or called her names, Jacob was to call the brother-in-law and both would take Daniel to his room, pin him down on his bed, and keep him immobilized for two hours. It was clear that this part of the program was bound to arouse strong opposition.

Daniel reacted well to the nonphysical parts of the program. He and his father began to develop some kind of dialogue during their daily ride. This new communication channel held some promise for the future. However, the pinning down proved to be a bad idea. When it was first applied, Daniel made such a commotion that a neighbor called the police. Luckily the police officer who arrived knew the family well; otherwise, the father might have been sent to jail. The officer told Daniel that if he wished, he could file a complaint of abuse against his father. Daniel chose not to take advantage of this option.

In spite of this incident, Daniel began to react positively. He was obviously enjoying his father's increased availability. However, one evening, Daniel came home with a radio he had bought from a friend. Jacob asked him how much he had paid and, deciding that it was not a fair price, ordered him to return the radio—immediately. This use of authority on an issue that was not perceived as legitimate by Daniel provoked a backlash. Daniel stayed out for the entire night. After a fruitless search. Jacob called the therapist and the school principal, the therapist called the head of the clinic, and the head of the clinic called the therapist supervisor. Nobody slept.

Daniel arrived in the morning and was immediately pinned down, this time with no resistance. The therapist called an emergency session with the parents and the following message was framed, to be solemnly delivered to Daniel.

> You did wrong not to return the radio last evening and further wrong not to come home. But we understand that you felt humiliated. This was not our purpose. We do not wish to humiliate you and will do our best to make sure that this doesn't happen again. You are a full citizen in this house. As such, you have to abide by its rules and laws. We will enforce the rules and the laws, but without humiliation. You will be a full citizen with full duties and full dignity.

The therapeutic theme became "boundaries without humiliation." Daniel was also told that there would be no more pinning down, because of the humiliation involved. Jacob's acknowledgment and his retreat from the offensive aspects of the program improved the atmosphere.

Within three weeks after the program started, both sides had been so weakened by the struggle that they were ripe for a compromise. The father agreed to send Daniel to a secular school and Daniel agreed to observe all religious edicts until he reached the age of 18, when he himself could decide on his religious course. From then on, Daniel accompanied his father to the synagogue every Saturday. A follow-up nine months later showed that the agreements had been kept and that Daniel was happy in his new school.

Case 13: "The Work of Despair"

Jason was as slippery as an eel: If a teacher angered him, he would vanish. If his parents, John and Lillian, refused to give him money, he would beg on the streets. If they dared to inquire as to where he had been, he would disappear and not return until late that night or the next day. If they warned him that he would find the door locked, he would ignore them and sleep on a park bench. At other times, he was highly explosive. At his previous school (from which he had been expelled a year earlier), his outbursts were talked of as events of almost mythic proportions. Jason spent most of his days with his friends in a video arcade. He begged for tokens and probably stole from unwary players. He was only 14, but everybody around him felt very old.

The one time that Jason's father had hit him, Jason went to the police and complained of abuse. John was arrested and jailed for a couple of days. Jason gloated: his father was now powerless against him. As if to prove that this was so, Jason hit John a number of times, and John, fearing another brush with the law, refused to protect himself. Jason was quite sure that his parents would, under no circumstances, file a complaint against him: they feared that if Jason were locked up, he would either commit suicide or become a full-fledged criminal.

Recently, Jason had sneaked into his former school, interrupting a class and gesturing obscenely. The police were called and Jason was assigned to a probation officer who, knowing of Jason's violence at school, recommended that he be sent to a reformatory. The judge, however, decided to give Jason another chance. John and Lillian came to therapy at this time, with the intention of doing all they could to keep Jason at home.

Jason was sure that his parents would always get him off the hook. He also believed that the teachers and officials at his new school would come to his aid. This belief was not unjustified. In effect, the school staff—led by a devoted counselor—went to great lengths to help him out. They allowed him to study when and with whom he wished. Out of consideration for his restlessness, he was also allowed to roam about freely on the school premises. Not surprisingly, he loafed most of the day. The program, although scholastically meaningless, at least decreased friction and there had been very few incidents in the new school. But the parents considered the program a Band-Aid response. They did not think that the school was accomplishing anything, but was merely buying some quiet by winking at Jason's real problems.

John was closer to Jason than Lillian was, and, despite the clashes, was a very caring father. Lillian confessed, in an agony of self-reproach, that her love for Jason was drying up. Despite the advice of another therapist that she show love under all circumstances, she felt she could not pretend. Jason complained that Lillian preferred his younger brother (age 9) and his sister (age 16) to him. Lillian knew how much Jason thirsted for her affection. Sometimes, he would actually ask her to hug and kiss him, although Lillian felt that this usually happened when he had done something wrong and wanted the hug and kiss as tokens of unconditional forgiveness. She was in a bind: if she gave in, she felt put upon; if she did not, she was a bad mother.

The therapist invited Jason to the second session together with the parents. At first, he seemed quite cooperative, but when the therapist raised the possibility of the parents' sitting with Jason every evening to plan for the next day, he protested in horror: "They may even want me to do homework!" The voices grew louder and Jason started to threaten. The therapist lost control and warned Jason that if he hit his father again, thinking himself safe because his father would be afraid of the police, he should expect the therapist to go to the police as well and tell the whole story. Later in the evening, Jason called the therapist and complained that his life had grown much worse since the session. He swore that he would never ever step into the therapist's office again. However, John and Lillian said they were glad that someone had taken their side: they even thought that the therapist's flare-up was part of the method!

Jason was, by now, spending all his time at the video arcade. The therapist suggested that the parents make surprise visits there. When they did so, Jason ran away and disappeared for the day. After three or four such visits, however, Jason started to reduce his loitering. He also went back to playing basketball (at which he had excelled in the past). When John went overseas on a business trip, Jason asked his father to bring him an expensive computer game. John phoned daily just to talk to Jason but making it clear that he was not buying the game. Lillian expected a crisis. Surprisingly, Jason was glad to have his father back in spite of the fact that he arrived with a small present (far less expensive than the game). At school, too, there had been only one bad incident in six weeks, an excellent record for Jason.

But in spite of these promising signs, Jason was not doing anything constructive. By now, his parents were ready to push for more. They came up with a modest, but determined, demand—that Jason spend half an hour a day with one of them, doing homework. At school, the counselor and teacher presented a similar demand: Jason should spend half an hour a day, working under supervision. Jason went on the warpath: he would vanish for entire nights, stopped informing his parents of his whereabouts, and became verbally abusive at home and violent at school. During one of these episodes, he frightened another boy so badly that the latter sought refuge in the principal's office for hours, trembling with fear and alleging that Jason's street friends were waiting outside to finish him off. When the staff tried to restrain him, Jason threatened a teacher with murder. The police were called and Jason struck at them. John and Lillian went to the station house to pick him up. Surprisingly, no charges were pressed.

After this incident, everybody was on the alert: the therapist received emergency calls from Lillian, the school principal, and the probation officer. The attempt to get Jason to study had led to an unbearable escalation in his violent behavior. The school wanted Jason out immediately. The probation officer thought there was no alternative but to place Jason in a reform school. The judge in charge of the care scheduled a hearing at which a decision on Jason's placement would be reached. Far from being cowed, however, he seemed all the more defiant.

John and Lillian asked the therapist if something could still be salvaged. They wondered if there was anything they could do that might have some effect on their son. Could the school be persuaded to try again with him? A meeting was convened with the probation officer, the school principal, John, and Lillian. Lillian cogently argued that Jason had not carried out any of the acts that are most typical of a juvenile delinquent: he had not used drugs, let alone been involved in drug traffic, and had not taken part in burglaries or other criminal activity. Time spent in a reformatory would, in all probability, toughen his attitude, rather than "reform" him. The therapist expressed the opinion that sending Jason to a reform school would, at this juncture, reflect the anger and the helplessness of the caretakers more than it would offer any real treatment option. He asked for a few days in which to come up with a new proposal.

After consulting with some colleagues, the therapist invited the parents to a session. He told them that, from Jason's perspective, there might be a big difference between being told by the parents what to do with himself and being told that they would act in self-protection. He proposed that the parents declare to Jason that they were giving up all positive guidance but would fight, all the more strongly, to protect themselves and the house from violence and blatant exploitation. The parents asked the therapist if this were not simply a confession of despair. The therapist told them that, in a sense, it was, but that it might be a constructive despair. The parents and therapist then composed the following message to Jason.

> *We have reached the conclusion that we cannot guide you or influence you in any positive sense. We cannot set you any model for action or have you live according to our standards. We cannot save you or rescue you. We accept that you cannot abide being guided or told what to do by us or by any other adult. We accept that for you being told what to do is tantamount to a total surrender. We will respect your position, because we know it cannot be changed. However, we will not be abused or exploited. We respect your limits and will have you respect ours. We won't tell you to study or to change your company of friends. However, there will be no violence of any kind at home. We won't tell you where to go, but you will have to tell us where you are. Barring this, we would feel exploited and we won't abide that.*

We call this program *the work of despair* (Omer & Rosenbaum, 1997): despair resulting from *their* illusions of influence and from *their* rescue fantasies. However, they were not despairing about Jason as a person. In the future, Jason might make his life decisions in a new way. Neither were they despairing about their ability to protect themselves from violence and exploitation. John and Lillian understood that they would have to work hard to free themselves from illusory hopes.

With the parents' agreement, the therapist brought a similar proposal to the school staff. All pretense would be given up: the staff members would tell Jason that they could not make him study, but he would only be allowed to stay in school while he was in class and busy with some school activity. The moment he decided to leave class, he would have to go home. If he resisted, the police would be called. The principal asked who would be legally responsible for Jason when he left the school during school hours. The therapist said that his parents would sign a statement to the effect that they would assume that responsibility. The therapist also told the staff about the parallel message that was being relayed to Jason by his parents. The staff's response was very positive. The therapist updated the probation officer on the plan, and he convinced the judge to postpone the hearing for another two months.

Jason reacted well. He would come to school and stay for a couple of hours—in class. Once he left his class, he was sent home. There were no more untoward incidents at school. The tension at home also subsided. However, after a month of quiet, he did something that was unacceptable to Lillian and John: he decided to have a ring inserted in his chin. Lillian and John felt that this was an affront they could not tolerate. Why, precisely, the ring should so arouse the parents' resistance is a bit of a mystery. They both maintained that they would feel bad if Jason went about in their house with a chin ring. They told him peremptorily that he would not be allowed in the house with the ring. Jason tried all his tricks to get his way. He even tried to enlist the help of the probation officer, arguing that his parents had no right to intervene in this matter.

As expected, he decided to flout his parents' prohibition and came home with the ring inserted. Lillian barricaded herself inside the house and refused him entrance. He knocked, raved, and threw stones at the window, but to no avail. He called John at work, but John was no less adamant. He asked Lillian to let him in and take the ring out by herself. She told him he would have to do it alone. After two hours, Jason went back to the doctor and had the ring removed. When he returned home, he did not even mention the episode.

Things were calm for the next two months. Jason started to interact more positively with Lillian. He even seemed to miss her sermonizing. He would mock her manner and say in a caricature of her tone of voice, "If you only did something constructive, you would meet with a fitting response from our side!" She would smile, but was not drawn in. He now spent most of his time at home, watching television, playing with his old computer games, and complaining of boredom. He seldom went to the video arcade.

When the hearing took place, John told the judge that he knew that he and Lillian had failed as parents and had nothing positive to offer Jason. If the court were to propose any truly positive program, he would collaborate. Lillian backed him up. The judge decided that there were no grounds for sending Jason to a reformatory.

During a final therapy session with the parents, John said that although Jason might not have been helped much, they had. They felt that their home had become a better place. Lillian added that she felt much better without pretenses and cosmetic solutions. Now Jason would have to face reality. Whether this will help him change, it is too soon to tell.

◆

Chapter Seven

Involving the Child in the Therapy

It is usually taken for granted, by parents and professionals alike, that the child must be personally involved in the therapy. This premise is not always valid when the goal is the establishment of parental presence; in this case, it is the parents who are the chief clients and agents of change. Routinely following the assumption that the child should be involved may have a detrimental effect on the therapy. For example, this happens if the child succeeds in monopolizing the sessions or utilizes the sessions as a source of information concerning the parents' plans so as to neutralize them. One might argue that it is the therapist's task to preclude this from happening. However, a good way to prevent these detrimental outcomes might be to keep the child away from the sessions.

However, when parents and child agree on a common goal, the child's involvement can be a boon for the therapy. There are also circumstances when it becomes imperative to get a therapeutic message across to the child. This happens when the parents and child evolve a strictly negative view of each other, a process that often leads to a negative spiral. The therapist and parents then search for a way of expressing respect for the rebel, which may help resolve the impasse and repair the damage.

Common Goals and Common Enemies

There is one phrase that could easily rank as *the most used and most useless* parental advice to children: "It is for your own good!" Parents keep repeating this refrain despite the fact that probably not a single child in history has ever replied: "Thanks, Dad and Mom! Now, I understand!" With time, many children discover that the parents' advice was actually not as bad as it seemed, but this belated recognition never seems to arrive when the parents are actively hammering, "It is for your own good!" If anything, the formula seems to have the opposite effect: the child no longer pays any attention to the parents.

Why do parents persevere? They do so because the prize is so valuable. Parents feel that if it were only possible to share their experiences with their children, the children's troubles would be over! However, we know that this does not happen. Parental wisdom is not really what children need. Children have to evolve their own wisdom, out of their own experiences and on their own terms. The parents' experiences are, of course, part of the stuff that children use in building their own experiences. But they are no more than raw material to be adapted and molded according to a particular child's understanding and needs. In addition, much of the parental raw material will end up being discarded as unsuitable to the times or to the child's interests and style.

Often the parents can hardly wait for the child to complete his or her slow work of selecting and assimilating the raw material they are offering. For example, if the child were given the right to experiment on his or her own with violence, drugs, delinquency, and sex, there might be little to salvage at the end of the experiment. Then it would be vital to convey the message, "It is for your own good!"

However, the question is how to bridge the barrier, rather than knocking against it again and again. In this respect, the therapist may have a role to play. Knowing that the parents' terms cannot be accepted as such by the child, the therapist can function as a translator and adapter in an attempt to create a common language and define a common goal.

There are many ways of facilitating parent–child communication and of furthering the pursuit of common goals. Some therapists focus on helping parents and children talk more openly and clearly. Others focus on developing a more empathic mutual perception. Still others work on the development of formal agreements. One highly original contribution in this area is that of Michael White and David Epson (1990), who evolved a procedure for personalizing the problem in the form of an enemy to be jointly fought by parents and child. In depicting the problem as a villain, White and Epston have developed a lively therapeutic language that seems to be equally acceptable to adults and children. It is as if a family Esperanto has been found.

Although the following case was decidedly influenced by White and Epston, the emphasis is on the recovery of parental authority. I and the therapist in charge (Uri Weinblatt) take full responsibility for any deviations from the original approach.

Case 14: Finding a "Good Enemy" to Fight Together

Morris and Daphne were at a loss to explain what had happened with their 13-year-old son. Matt had been a brilliant boy admired by all, but his marks and school performance had fallen so much, and his image had become so tarnished, that almost everybody, including his parents, had serious doubts about his mental capacity. The school had recommended that Matt be transferred to one more appropriate to his low accomplishments.

After many attempts to make Matt study, the parents had only achieved more arguments and less cooperation. His negative be-

117

havior was also spreading to new areas: he now refused to get up in the morning and often arrived home very late at night. In their consultations with Matt's teachers, Morris and Daphne were shocked to find that they spoke about Matt in a dismissive tone. Matt felt the same about the staff: he described them as trash and behaved toward them accordingly. Lately, he had begun to eat during class, sometimes he would get up and leave, without a word of explanation, in the middle of a lesson.

Daphne had tried the strict approach and Morris the soft one, both to no avail, although Matt was still courteous toward his parents when no demands were made. However, when the slightest expectations were raised, Matt would react with open contempt. The only person he consistently respected was his older brother, a pilot in the air force.

The therapist asked the parents to bring Matt along with them for the second session. When asked whether he disliked the school's attitude toward him, Matt said he did. With a little prompting, Matt complained that the teachers were "on his case." The therapist asked whether the teachers were aware of his capabilities. He answered that they thought little of him, but that he didn't care. The therapist then asked Matt and his parents if there were other people who had been adversely affected by this negative opinion and now thought less well of Matt than in the past. Matt admitted that some of his friends had lower opinions of him, and the parents confessed that they also, sometimes, respected Matt less than before and believed less in his abilities. The therapist then asked Matt if he ever doubted his own abilities and his chances for success. Matt said that, yes, he was doubtful about himself.

The therapist concluded that a growing wave of disparagement was affecting and contaminating everybody. *Disparagement* had gradually convinced the teachers that Matt was less capable than he was. *Disparagement* had also caused Matt's friends, relatives, and parents to doubt his abilities. It seemed that Matt also, at least sometimes, fell into the trap of *Disparagement* by believing that his chances for success were quite low. *Disparagement* was thus getting everybody into its bag. Matt and his parents soon joined in this new way of talking, referring to *Disparagement* as if it were an entity.

The therapist ventured that one of *Disparagement's* dirtiest tricks was to convince Matt that it was his friend. Thus, by helping Matt to disparage others, *Disparagement* gave him the illusion that it was helping him. This, however, was exactly what *Disparagement* wanted, as Matt's disparagement of others had the effect of strengthening their disparagement of him. Then it was only a matter of time until the poison would creep under Matt's own skin. In turn, his parents also felt that their lives were being affected by *Disparagement*: they felt worse about themselves and about Matt; there were more disputes and less family feeling.

When the therapist inquired as to whether there had been any occasions on which *Disparagement* had suffered a partial or temporary defeat at the hands of Matt and his parents, they indicated that there indeed had been a number of times when they had maintained a positive attitude of mutual respect, in spite of all the attempts of *Disparagement* to trick them.

The therapist asked Matt whether he was interested in using the two months that were left to the end of the semester for an all-out fight against *Disparagement*. He was told that he might think of this as an experiment: once he had shown his worth, he could decide how he preferred to live in the future. Matt liked the idea. The therapist said that since time was short, if he really wanted to do it, he would have to become ready for a tough fight, involving very serious training. Matt did not answer. The therapist said that since the fight might be too hard for Matt and his parents to take on, he would give them a couple of days to think things over. To help them weigh the proposal, he lent them a video about people who had decided that they would do all they could to fight not only against disparagement, but also against hatred and contempt. The film was *The Dirty Dozen.*

Matt returned ready for battle. However, the parents wondered why the therapist had wanted them to watch that particular film since it was about criminals. The therapist explained that he had chosen it because the criminals had redeemed their criminal deeds by their strenuous efforts and their devotion. Matt had, of course, done nothing that was morally wrong. And yet, in the coming weeks, his willpower and determination also would be put to a serious test.

Thus, Matt would have to wake up very early each morning and his parents would have to make sure that he did so. As in *The Dirty Dozen*, the major crisis would probably arrive with the first punishment: the trainee had to decide whether to give up or to clench his teeth and go ahead. If Matt was not ready to take the punishment, it might be better if he said so right now, as the whole effort would then be useless. Matt said he would hold on.

The rest of the session was devoted to the selection of a team of high-level trainers. The parents would be in charge of the home routine and of contacting the three private teachers who were chosen for the most difficult subjects (math, history, and English). Morris proposed that he would go jogging with Matt every evening. Matt's brother would plan a physical fitness program for him. Daphne would help Matt prepare daily graphs to detail his goals and progress.

After five good days, Matt refused to get up one morning. His father confiscated half of his CDs. When Matt complained, Morris said he would not give in to *Disparagement* without a fight. Matt clenched his teeth and swallowed the punishment. The results were good. At school, Matt failed one exam but did very well on the rest. He still thought, however, that two of the teachers had it in for him. The parents also thought that the school's attitude toward Matt was still negative. Matt wanted to go to another school. The parents decided to check whether, with his new marks, he might not be accepted by a school with higher standards than his present one. He was accepted.

Respect for Rebels

If gaining the child as an ally is a boon for therapy, dealing with the extreme negative views that develop between parents and child—sometimes as a side effect of the very struggle for parental presence—is a must. As we have seen, issues of dignity are usually at the center of such impasses. If the therapist then succeeds in conveying, directly or through the parents, a convincing message of respect for the rebel-child, the crisis may become an opportunity. However, the respect must not weaken the parents or abet the child's destructive acts.

One might question the good of expressing respect for the rebel, when the parents are striving to subdue the rebellion. Shouldn't one wait until the struggle is over? However, waiting is useless when it is precisely the negative view that prevents all positive developments. Conveying a respectful view of the rebel may reverse the negative escalation.

One might still argue that respect for the child must not entail respect for the rebel within the child. The parents perhaps could say, "I respect you, but condemn your rebellion!" But to whom does the "you" in the parental message refer? When parent and child labor vainly in mutual hostility, the rebel becomes the parents' whole image of the child. Saying "I respect you but condemn the rebel in you!" really means "I respect the child you should or used to be, but not the one you are!" This is the same as showing no respect at all. What is needed, instead, is to give an actual meaning to the assertion of respect.

Respect for the rebel must not, however, entail an endorsement of the child's destructive acts. Rather, the object of respect is the legitimate striving that underlies the rebellion. Such an account of a person's behavior is what we call an *empathic narrative*

121

(Omer, 1997). The person's acts are described as making good sense—so much so, that, under similar circumstances, we could view ourselves as acting likewise. With the rebellious child, the empathic narrative presents an inside glimpse at the rebellion. What looks, from the outside, absurd and irrational, now looks, from the inside, as a justifiable attitude.

How is the empathic narrative conveyed? Who delivers it to the child? Sometimes the parents do, if they truly and fully agree with the new description. Sometimes, however, the parents fear that the child will interpret their words as a sign of weakness, or the deadlock may be such that they feel that the child will not listen to whatever they say. The therapist can then step in, as a third party, and relay the message (in person or by letter). The child then comes to participate (even if only as a passive recipient) in the therapy and, at least temporarily, a triad (parent–child–therapist) is instituted that may be less prone to impasse than the original parent–child dyad.

To safeguard the parents' standing, the empathic description of the rebellion should be followed by an empathic description of the parents' attitude. It is hoped that this double positive description will replace the mutual denigration. Sometimes, although a full reconciliation cannot be achieved, at least the mutual vilification is abrogated. At other times, however, parental respect meets with full filial respect and parental presence with filial presence.

Case 15: A Double Empathic Narrative: Respecting the Rebel and the Jailer

At the age of 14, Mike returned to Israel with his father, Richard. His mother had smuggled him out of the country after her divorce, without his father's knowledge. He grew up in France, feeling lonesome and different. It took him a long time to learn the language and the other children always made fun of his for-

eign accent and manners. He missed his old home and, in a surprising way for a child, assumed the demeanor of an exile.
Although he was very intelligent, his schoolwork was poor.
Things gradually got worse: at the age of 12, after having played
truant for weeks, he was transferred to a special school for children with behavior problems.

At 14, he ran away from home, slept in a park, and managed
to evade the search parties for two weeks. He joined a bunch of
street kids and made friends with the homeless. He began to think
of himself as belonging with these people. He started to smoke
and drink and twice was arrested for theft. His mother panicked
and phoned his father, asking him to take Mike to Israel. However, Mike had lost his onetime yearning for his old home and
only agreed to a trial visit after he was promised that he could
decide where he wanted to live. He was soon disabused of this
illusion: after one month in Israel, when he said he wanted to go
back to France, Richard told him that he had agreed with his
mother that Mike would stay in Israel. So far as Mike was concerned, he had been kidnapped for the second time.

Richard brought Mike to therapy after he ran away from
home. Once again, he slept on a beach for a week, consorting
with homeless people. He was drunk when his father found him.
Richard needed little prodding from the therapist to keep close
watch over Mike. For the duration of the summer vacation, he
never left Mike alone. To this end, he made far-reaching changes
in his work routine. He kept Mike from smoking, drinking, and
meeting with the "wrong" people. He also supervised his appearance, by picking out his clothes and making sure that he
showered regularly. Mike protested, but made no new attempts
to run away. After a month, he even started to help Richard with
his work as a carpenter. Mike explained that, for him, this was
not work, since he only did things that gave him pleasure. He
espoused a marginal and hedonist philosophy: work and duty
were the values of the herd; he would stand by the side, associate

only with other nonconformists, and indulge his pleasure. He wrote surrealistic poems, philosophized, and daydreamed. He talked of one day owning a "kinky" nightclub that would bring him money and allow him to meet the kind of people he liked.

Mike made his principled opposition to his "incarceration" apparent in myriad ways: he spoke derisively to Richard and his wife, scoffed at their values, was a nuisance in the house, and succeeded in getting expelled from his new school after attending it for a month. He made no friends and dared the adults to try to change him. He knew that the law was on their side, but only for as long as he was a minor. Until then, he would do time but would allow his jailers no illusions about him. Richard was determined to go on watching over Mike, even if he had to sacrifice four years to the task. He would be content with nothing less than getting Mike to act and study like a normal kid and to acknowledge to his father that all was being done for his sake.

Initially, the therapist saw Mike and Richard together. Their positions, however, seemed irreconcilable. After three months of therapy, the following message was delivered when both were present, in an attempt to overcome the stalemate.

> *Mike, I want to tell you how I think you became who you are. The circumstances of your life have turned you into an outcast. This was through no choice of yours and it was true long before you began your open rebellion. You suffered from this condition throughout your childhood. Then, I don't know exactly when, you made the creative decision to take on the identity of the outcast. This rescued you from being helpless and miserable. It was as if you were saying, "You cast me out, so I cast you out! You banish me, so I banish you! Get out of my world!" Being an exile became your badge of honor and your life philosophy. From being scoffed at, you became the scoffer: the conformists, the nice guys, and the herd are the ones to be despised. With this existential choice, you have also evolved a*

survival kit with two ruling attitudes: provocation and disqualification. When you provoke, you are no longer the victim. When you disqualify others, they become inferior. In your realm, the outcast is king.

You also found other outcasts whom you could join, as an equal. They became more important for you than the whole world. You miss them, as you once missed your old home, and you want to join them, no matter what others may think. These attitudes, however absurd they may seem to others, redeemed you from your unbearable condition as a kidnapped, helpless, and lowly victim.

However, you are also paying a price. You know that your lifestyle is dangerous and that it could kill you. From your survivorship, I gather that you would rather keep your achievements as an identity but also go on living. I hope you can do both.

I can see three possible paths for your future. The first is the path of conformity. This is closed, so far as you are concerned. Although your father may still want you to get back on it, you know better. For you, it would mean accepting the others' right to despise and reject you, while, at the same time, having to beg for their favor. I mention this path, not because there is any danger that you may take it, but because it is still a source of external pressure on you. You know that however much your father may pressure you, he cannot and will not change you.

The second is the path of death, which means your total rejection of any option that is offered to you. Paradoxically, by choosing this path, you not only may be killing yourself physically, but also may be killing your freedom, because then you have no freedom of choice, but only to do the opposite of what others tell you. I feel that sometimes you want to take this path, but at other times, it feels too narrow and uncreative. In effect, when you write poetry or when you do something out of pure pleasure, and not simply because it is the contrary of what others say, you are actually walking away from the death path.

This points in the direction of the third path: the path of rugged individuality. The essence of this path is to develop your identity as an outsider, while overcoming all dangers to survival. Thus, when you fantasize about opening a kinky nightclub, you are cherishing your individuality. You remain an outcast from the point of view of "normal society" while, at the same time, nurturing your own free options.

I want to be honest with you about how I view your father's role. I think that, just like you, he cannot act otherwise. I would call him the devoted jailer. He is a jailer, no doubt, but one who is different from those whom you usually meet. Like you, he is fighting his own existential battle. If he were to give in, he would feel as if he were, retrospectively, agreeing to your mother's kidnapping, to his own deprivation of a son and to your deprivation of a father. His is the path of self-loyalty. Anything else would be crass self-betrayal. Of course, you protest, for it is your duty to do so. Of course, you must promise yourself never to give in, for this is crucial to your sense of worth. To my mind, however, your father may be contributing to your project of rugged individuality: he gives you the experience of devotion, which you will need as part of your personal armamentarium. When you finally get your freedom, at the age of 18, you will probably be better able to make use of it, having had this experience. He is also giving you the strongest possible training in sticking to your inner direction. For if you do so in spite of his continuous shadowing, you will have proved yourself a very tough rebel.

As the message was read, Mike turned to his father again and again, almost begging him to understand. This attitude was very different from his usual dismissive one. They were both moved and it took a while for them to compose themselves.

In the coming weeks, there were no significant changes in Mike's interaction with his father. Gradually, however, he became more involved in his new school, his marks improved, and he never played truant. Ostensibly, his attitude remained unchanged. Thus, although he declared that he was not actually in therapy, because he was brought in under duress, he was very glad to talk to the therapist about his ideas and to read him his poems. Sometimes, the therapist, like the father, would become frustrated because Mike refused to say he needed help. However, the therapist told Mike that on second thought, he understood that he was mistaken in expecting him to take on the identity of a patient. This would be tantamount to a surrender.

The message was also important for Mike's father. It helped him to accept the necessary hardships and to give up any illusions about Mike's full acceptance of his values. In a way, the empathic narrative had helped Richard become, not only a devoted jailer, but also a respectful one.

Case 16: An Empathic Narrative in a Life-Threatening Impasse

Up until the age of 21, Jerry had been healthy. Then, in a matter of weeks, his life completely changed. He discovered blood in his urine, and severe kidney insufficiency was diagnosed. The disease progressed with lightning speed and within a month, Jerry had lost both kidneys and been sent abroad to undergo a transplant. His father, George, had been the key figure in the process of decisionmaking. Were it not for his promptness and devotion, Jerry might have lost his life. George was also Jerry's chief support throughout his convalescence. His mother, Clara, took care of the household (she had three younger children) and the family business, while her husband was away with Jerry. She was glad that George had assumed the more painful role.

After the operation, Jerry's first question to the surgeon was whether he would be able to father children. His later behavior showed that he was actually worried about his sexual potency. Back at home, he developed a style of living geared to pleasure and sex. He gave up his plans to attend college, dismissed all suggestions about work, spent his nights at clubs and bars, and brought home one young woman after another. This routine persisted for a year. He practically took over his father's car. His father had to notify him beforehand if he wanted to use it. Jerry wheedled the money for his escapades mainly from George. But this was not enough, Jerry wanted a car of his own and kept pressuring his father to buy him one. When George refused, Jerry castigated him for putting money before his son's life. He felt he was the most luckless youth on earth. How could his parents fail to understand that he deserved some compensation for his ill-starred fate?

Jerry had to follow a strict medical regimen. Lack of compliance with the prescribed dosage of medication, or even irregularities in its timing, might have dangerous consequences. Jerry made light of the demanding schedule, often failing to take the pills unless his father was there to make sure that he did so. George thus became Jerry's medical caretaker. He woke him every morning (sometimes immediately after Jerry had gone to sleep, having just returned from his nightly spree) to give him the pills. Jerry was usually so tired that it would take minutes of vigorous shaking before he was ready to swallow his medicine. The car became the pawn in the battles over medical compliance: George would threaten not to give him the car unless he cooperated, whereas Jerry would become more and more neglectful unless George promised him the car unconditionally. Jerry kept his father teetering on the verge of terror. Thus, he might leave his pills inside the car on a hot summer day, declare he no longer would take the medication and would turn to a macrobiotic diet, or would disappear, without the pills. He would justify these actions by his despair at not having a car of his own.

The more George pleaded, the more irresponsibly Jerry behaved. George, however, could not trust Jerry to take care of himself, even for a short time. The two became caught up in a cat-and-mouse game. Each talked to and about the other in a highly negative way. George said that Jerry was irrational, irresponsible, and ungrateful. Jerry said that he had no parents, that they had never tried to understand him, and that under the pretext of care, they were leading him into despair. George would try to explain to him that it was all for his own good. Jerry would indicate he was sick of this refrain. Clara despaired of both: Jerry was disgusting and George was a sucker.

This was the dilemma that the parents presented to the therapist in the first interview. For them, it seemed a no-win situation. The therapist thought there was little chance of progress, as long as both sides held such negative views of each other. In an attempt to loosen the deadlock, the therapist opened the second session, which also included Jerry, by reading the family the following message.

I want to share with you my thoughts about your situation. First of all, I want to tell you that I don't think that Jerry's behavior is senseless. On the contrary, I think it is a meaningful attempt to deal with an extreme situation.

Jerry, you have met death face to face. In a sense, the meeting is not over, for the risk of death is still with you and will remain with you for a long time. You feel, rightly, that fate has dealt you a very bad card and you are expected not only to go on living under a perpetual threat, but also to be a good boy and comply fully with the imposed conditions, humbly begging the gods to pity you and prolong your lease.

Your reaction, as I understand it, is a complete rejection of the terms. You don't stop saying, "I will go on living to the full! I won't give in and I won't be curbed!" Your first question to the surgeon, when you woke up, was "Will I be able to father

129

children?" I think that what you actually meant was, "Will I be able to love and have a real sex life?" The answer soon came. You can and you will! It is as if you were answering fate, your would-be tyrant; "See how I surrender!"

Your lifestyle is a defiant show of vitality: "I will not live for a hypothetical future but here and now!" I respect your courage, your aliveness, and your protest. You are a hero of the present. Many people would envy your audacity and dream about living as you do.

However, there is another side to the medal that is crucial for your parents, if not for you. I want to speak for this side as clearly as I spoke for yours. Your gamble is a game of Russian roulette. Each day offers a possible new win as well as a new risk. You say, "So I must take my pill exactly at 7:00? I will take it when I am ready! If my father thinks otherwise, it's his problem!" or "So I must sleep regular hours each night? I will go to sleep when the fun is over!" Actually, you have chosen to live until the bullet in your game is in the barrel. This may happen tomorrow, or in a couple of years. In a sense, your Russian roulette is the roulette of despair, for your basic assumption is that with the gift you've received from the hands of fate, there is no meaning in the future. You did not submit to fate in its demand that you live in fear and trembling. But you did submit to fate in giving up your future without a fight. Actually, you have signed an old contract with the devil: "I pledge you my future! But today, let me paint the town red!"

Your parents may understand, and perhaps respect, the meaning of your choice. What they cannot do, however, is comply with it. If they do so, they will be signing your death warrant with their own hands. If they follow you in that direction, they will never be able to forgive themselves. They have asked for my help. It became clear, after five minutes of talk, that they feel as if they themselves were pushing the bullet into your gun barrel. I will try my best to help them stop the roulette. If your *decision wipes away your future, they must not abet it, under any circumstances! What is so meaningful to you is sheer hell for them. They asked me if you might try to commit suicide if they stopped giving in to you. I said there was such a risk. I do not think you ever made an empty threat. I am sure you have not, because you play the game of life and death daily, so that you are at the brink in innumerable day-to-day situations. I will try to help them do all they can to prevent you from killing yourself, except for one thing: giving in to your demands. For if they do so, they will be guaranteeing your end. I respect you and I can identify with the awful weight of your tragedy. For this reason, I do not doubt your seriousness. But I think your parents simply cannot afford to give in to you. Otherwise, you have no chance at all.*

So what am I proposing? That you accept the dictate of fate and start living as a nice boy and obedient pupil? This is not my intention. You dared to say "No!" to fate. Maybe you will also find the daring to demand both the present and the future. Your adventurous style will not leave you. It is part of you. It is one of your achievements. You are in no danger of becoming a "mother's boy." The question now is whether you will also stop being fate's sucker in another respect by refusing to surrender your future to it. I will continue meeting with your parents. I will meet with anybody who cares about you. I will be glad if you join us. Not because I want to treat your "psychological problems," but so that we may honestly think about how you can continue to live in the present without giving your life in exchange.

Five minutes after reading the letter, the therapist made a mistake. Struck by the message's enormous impact, he decided to forge ahead, proposing that the parents should stop Jerry's generous allowance and use of the car. This declaration had the effect of almost wiping out Jerry's positive emotional reaction. For the rest of the session, Jerry raved and threatened. The days that followed, however, showed that not all was lost. Jerry was helpful and considerate as never before. In the coming sessions (with the parents alone), George learned to change his ineffective parental rhetoric ("It is all for your own good!"). For a while, things seemed to be going better. Jerry started to work (unfortunately, only for a while) and stopped asking for money (but not for the car).

In the following months, there were many ups and downs. George did not feel he could just give up his caretaking role. The ties between George and Jerry would have to change very gradually. Some steps were made in this direction, allowing George and Clara their first vacation since the transplant. The therapist tried to help George transfer some of his caretaking functions to Clara, but with no success. George simply felt that he could not afford to give up the supervision. Jerry, for his part, continued his old lifestyle. When the therapist last met with the family, Jerry was planning to go to college. In addition, he had been badly frightened by the results of his latest medical examination and might be starting to accept the guidance of the hospital staff. This would, eventually, relieve George of his impossible duty. The therapist, however, felt that the situation was still explosive. He was not sure that the family would approach him in a new crisis. All in all, the message's impact had gradually worn off.

This case was a therapeutic failure. In contrast to even the most difficult cases presented here, absolutely no improvement was evident in spite of months of treatment. Nor was the path of resignation a viable alternative for this family: Who could become resigned to the threatened loss of a child's life? The choice of this case as the final one in the book was not meant to discourage the reader. In many other cases, children were rescued from suicidal lifestyles. However, to be able to help, we must also have the courage to face our limitations and to accept our failures without blaming others.

Conclusion

At the start of this book, I proposed three criteria for evaluating our concept: (1) that it offer us a practical guideline, (2) that it serve as a bridge between different approaches, and (3) that it be morally acceptable and easily discernible from authority based on naked power. To what extent have we accomplished this?

Parental Presence as a Practical Guideline

Parental presence has proved to be a handy concept—easy to grasp and apply. It is distinct from many other complex theoretical concepts, and it effectively brings to mind a rich gallery of images: the parent bear-hugging the child; sitting for hours in the child's room; preventing the child from hurting himself or herself; getting in touch with the child, even in odd ways and places; getting in touch with the people who are in touch with the child; spreading a net of people to protect the child. The gallery also shows counterinstances of parental presence—that is, parental absence: such as the parent's hitting the child; sending the child away; giving in to the child to buy peace and quiet; threatening, exhorting, and begging the child; sabotaging the spouse.

These images serve as a quick reference guide for practitioners and parents. Many an emergency will call to mind one or more of these pictures. The images are not, necessarily, to be applied literally. In many cases, considerable modification is needed. But this is precisely what is meant by a practical guideline: It provides us with a basic model that can be adapted to changing circumstances.

Parental Presence as a Theoretical Bridge for Different Approaches

The behavioral, systemic, and humanist contributions have enriched our thinking about parental presence. Conversely, through the converging lens of parental presence, we have enriched our view of the three approaches and of their contact points. Thus, we have seen that (1) the behavioral model touches on the systemic (for example, in the circular causation of the coercive pattern and in the importance attributed to systemic support); (2) the systemic touches on the humanist (systemic support affects the parents' sense of self); and (3) the humanist touches on the behavioral (the parents' inner resonance with the behavioral program, for example, may explain long-term maintenance or dropping out).

Parental presence thus turns out to be a three-way bridge: one may enter it from any theoretical direction and cross over to the others. This common-language quality is also shown in practice: the concept has proved highly acceptable to workers from different spheres, invariably facilitating dialogue and joint planning.

Personal Presence Versus Naked Power

In personal presence, the source of power and the moral justification are one and the same: the parents become strong by being there. It is by their willingness to care for the child with the whole of their bodily, emotional, and moral beings that the parents gain their influence and stature. Parental presence is thus the very opposite of the tyrannical power whose might comes from punishing, hitting, and banishing the child and whose goal is to prevent, rather than establish, intimacy. The tyrannical parent strives for distance. The present parent strives for contact.

Are we encouraging parental overinvolvement? Let us not forget that we are talking about families characterized by virtual parental absence. The child who rules by threats and violence needs the parents present and not simply more leeway for self-destruction. Gradually, as the child develops self-control, the parents and child will be able to evolve more symbolic ways of manifesting contact. In this connection, I would like to remark that in none of our cases did the parents go on practicing the bear hug, the sit-in, or very close personal shadowing as a matter of routine. Unlike arbitrary might, parental presence requires too much investment to be addictive in and of itself.

The workings of parental presence contrast deeply with those of naked power with respect to the child's dignity, as well. The goal of parental presence is never unconditional surrender. In effect, parental presence is an imminently dialogic concept: the parent strives to become present *for* the child and *in relation* to the child. This dialogic aspect is evident in many of the treatment's elements, such as in taking care to avoid humiliation, in being ready to give top priority to situations of impasse, and in emphasizing flexible authority. Most of all, however, the dialogic nature of the concept is evident in our expression of respect for the rebel. Actually, respect for the rebel, which we discussed in the last chapter, is the counterpart of respect for the parent, with which we began this book. I believe we have come full circle.

References

Amit, H. (1997). *Parents as human beings* (in Hebrew). Sifriat HaPoalim.

Anderson, L. M. (1969). Personality characteristics of parents of neurotic, aggressive and normal preadolescent boys. *Journal of Consulting and Clinical Psychology, 33,* 575–581.

Baumrind, D. (1971). Current patterns of parental authority. *Developmental Psychology Monographs, 4* (1, Pt. 2).

Baumrind, D. (1991). Effective parenting during the early adolescent transition. In P. A. Cowan & E. M. Petherington (Eds.), *Family transitions* (pp. 11–163). Hillsdale, NJ: Erlbaum.

Caplan, P. J. (1986, October). Take the blame off mother. *Psychology Today,* p. 70.

Chamberlain, P. & Patterson, G. R. (1995). Discipline and child compliance in parenting. In M. H. Bornstein (Ed.), *Handbook of parenting (Vol. 1)* (pp. 205–225). Mahwah, NJ: Erlbaum.

Elizur, Y. & Minuchin, S. (1993). *Institutionalizing madness.* Cambridge, MA: Harvard University Press.

References

Elson, M. (1984). Parenthood and the transformations of narcissism. In R. S. Cohen, B. J. Cohler, & S. H. Weissman (Eds.), *Parenthood: A psychodynamic perspective* (pp. 297–314). New York: Guilford.

Glenn, N. D. & McLanahan, S. (1982). Children and marital happiness: A further specification of the relationship. *Journal of Marriage and the Family, 44,* 63–72.

Haley, J. (1980). *Leaving home.* New York: McGraw-Hill.

Henggeler, S. W. (1996). *Family therapy and beyond.* Pacific Grove, CA: Brooks/Cole.

Henggeler, S. W., Rodick, J. D., Borduin, C. M., Hanson, C. L., Watson, S. M., & Urey, J. R. (1986). Multisystemic treatment of juvenile offenders: Effects on adolescent behavior and family interaction. *Development Psychology, 22,* 132–141.

Içami Tiba (1996). *Disciplina: Limite na medida certa.* Sao Paulo, Brazil: Editora Gente.

Kolvin, I., Miller, F. J. W., Fleeting, M., & Kolvin, P. A. (1988). Social and parenting factors affecting criminal-offence rates: Findings from the Newcastle Thousand Family Study (1947–1980). *British Journal of Psychiatry, 152,* 80–90.

Le Masters, E. E. & DeFrain, J. (1989). *Parents in contemporary America: A sympathetic view.* Belmont, CA: Wadsworth.

Minuchin, S. (1974). *Families and family therapy.* Cambridge, MA: Harvard University Press.

Omer, H. (1997). Narrative empathy. *Psychotherapy, 34,* 19–27.

Omer, H. (1998). Using therapeutic splitting to create empathic narratives. In M. F. Hoyt (Ed.), *The handbook of constructive therapies.* San Francisco: Jossey-Bass.

Omer, H. & Alon, N. (1997). *Constructing therapeutic narratives.* Northvale, NJ: Jason Aronson.

Omer, H. & London, P. (1988). Metamorphosis in psychotherapy: The end of the systems era. *Psychotherapy, 25,* 171–180.

Omer, H. & Rosenbaum, R. (1997). Diseases of hope and the work of despair. *Psychotherapy, 34,* 225–232.

Patterson, G. R. (1979). A performance theory for coercive family interactions. In R. Cairns (Ed.), *Social interaction: Methods, analysis and illustration* (pp. 119–162. Eugene, OR: Castalia.

Patterson, G. R. (1980). Mothers: The unacknowledged victims. *Monograph of the Society for Research in Child Development, 186, 45* (5), 1–47.

Patterson, G. R. (1982). *A social learning approach: Coercive family process.* Eugene, OR: Castalia.

Patterson, G. R., Reid, J. B., & Dishion, T. J. (1992). *Antisocial boys.* Eugene, OR: Castalia.

Price, J. (1997). *Power and compassion.* New York: Guilford.

Rollins, B. C. & Feldman, H. (1970). Marital satisfaction over the family life cycle. *Journal of Marriage and the Family, 32,* 20–28.

Straus, M. A. & Gelles, R. J. (1986). Societal change and change in family violence from 1975 to 1985 as revealed by two national surveys. *Journal of Marriage and the Family, 48,* 465–479.

White, L. K., Booth, A., & Edwards, J. N. (1986). Children and marital happiness: Why the negative correlation? *Journal of Family Issues, 7,* 131–147.

White, M. & Epston, D. (1990). *Narrative means to therapeutic ends.* New York: Norton.

Wilson, H. (1987). Parental supervision re-examined. *British Journal of Criminology, 27,* 215–301.

Winnicott, D. W. (1958). Hate in the countertransference. *Collected papers.* London: Tavistock

Winnicott, D. W. (1965). *The maturational process and the facilitating environment.* New York: International Universities Press.

Index

Index

Index